GUIDED MEDITATIONS, EXPLORATIONS AND HEALINGS

.

STEPHEN LEVINE

GATEWAY BOOKS, BATH

Published by
GATEWAY BOOKS
The Hollies, Wellow,
Bath BA2 8QJ

Copyright © 1991 by Stephen Levine

First British Edition 1993
Reprinted 1995

Cover design by Studio B, Bristol
Cover photo by Kevin Redpath

Printed and bound in Great Britain by
Redwood Books, Trowbridge, Wiltshire

British Cataloguing in Publication Data:
A catalogue record for this book is
available from the British Library.

ISBN 0-946551-85-5

CONTENTS

*To my mother and my father, who lived long enough to
see this work begin, and who died, after so many years of
confusion and separation, in my arms*

_____

Also by Stephen Levine

GRIST FOR THE MILL (with Ram Dass)

A GRADUAL AWAKENING

MEETINGS AT THE EDGE

WHO DIES?

HEALING INTO LIFE AND DEATH

FOREWORD

When our publishers first suggested that Ondrea and I collect into one volume the most widely used guided meditations and techniques for developing a healing awareness, which had been spread over the past twenty years through numerous articles and several books, we thought it was a good idea. So we put aside writing our manuscript on relationships as a path of awakening to undertake what seemed a simple enough task. But because the work is expanding so rapidly and many new guided meditations had been developed and much of the earlier material had evolved considerably, this became a much more extensive and intensive enterprise. A considerable amount of new material had arisen. And much of the earlier techniques had become distilled in the years of practice, counseling and workshops since their original publication. Indeed, the Opening the Heart of the Womb Meditation, which had begun as a single practice, has "matured" into three individual, progressive meditations. Also, new Loving Kindness, Mindfulness, Soft Belly, Pain, Grief, Healing, Eating, Resistance, and Dying meditations are offered here in print for the first time. And so, as it turns out, is most of the material in this book. Since it is our intention to offer something of a workbook of the techniques developed while teaching meditation and working with the healing and the dying, those acquainted with our previous books—*A Gradual Awakening, Who Dies?, Meetings at the Edge,* and *Healing into Life and Death*—will find a few of these meditations, and many of these ideas, familiar but much evolved from their original incarnations. This book is meant to be a culmination and distillation of these "technologies of the heart" and we offer them as experiments in the "healing we took birth for."

INTRODUCTION

There are many remarkable psychological and healing processes currently available, but none will do what a meditation practice can to lead you toward your deepest truth. And all could be enhanced by its deeper clarity and strength. As Freud said, "The best I can do is exchange your neurotic misery for ordinary human unhappiness." That "ordinary human unhappiness" is our common everyday grief. But this healing work we have taken birth to complete is to meet that grief in mercy and loving kindness instead of fear and self-hatred. Indeed, we can work endlessly in the mind to undo the tangle of conditioning that so twists and turns our lives. And this has considerable value, but don't stop there. The mind is only a part of our enormity. The mind insists on resolution and suffers intense confusion. But the heart requires only an integration of our pain into the vastness of our true nature. Indeed the psychological dilemma that draws our attention by the suffering it produces can be healed more readily in the heart of mercy than in the mind of fear and judgment.

As the mind turns toward the heart, subtle whispers are heard. Subtler aspects of existence are experienced. And there arises in the mind the question, "How do I go deeper?"

This book is organized in such a manner that the Loving Kindness meditation is the first offered. This is not a random selection, but offers the foundation for inner, as well as outer, practice. In the development of this meditation considerable concentration is gathered by connecting a heart-whispered wish for well-being with the rhythm of the breath. The cultivation of this heartful concentration leads to a deepening, merciful awareness; the basis of a spiritual/healing practice.

Using this meditation is a skillful way to develop the concentration necessary for the exploration that liberates consciousness. It is this quality of concentration that takes the diffused light of the mind and focuses it to a brilliance capable of illuminating even the subtlest nuance of each mind-moment passing. Such concentration allows awareness to remain focused on the moment and the tasks at hand. It is the quality most refer to when we speak of "mental strength."

At one point in my practice a teacher gave me a blue kasina (a meditation disc) to concentrate on for several hours a day in order to sharpen my capacity to focus. The object was not to "see the circle" but rather to "become the blue unwaveringly." A few weeks into this practice I met an old healer friend and as we hugged she commented, "When I hug you all I see is blue!" I thought to myself, "Why am I meditating on a blue kasina when my energies could be just as strongly concentrated by using a Loving Kindness meditation, and emanate an essential mercy so needed in the world, instead of a slight aberration in the mental decor?"

As one begins to use the Loving Kindness meditation as a means of concentrating the mind in the heart, or perhaps more accurately the heart *of* the mind (the essence of being, pure awareness), the words are quite helpful. "May I be happy. May I be free from suffering. May I be at peace." The words are a means of turning toward oneself with a care and well-being we seldom experience, particularly *from* ourselves. It is a whole new ball game. And the game is not as easy to play or as one-sided as we had hoped. There is much within us that arises to block that inner-directed mercy. Self-judgement. Fear. Doubt. Deep negations. And so the words find their track riding on the breath. The mind becomes focused by the words and sensitized by the moment-to-moment awareness of the breath. The breath and the words merge in the heart to draw the mind toward clarity and a healing kindness.

Awareness creates a sense of presence. Concentration intensifies that sense. The more concentrated the mind, the deeper the calm, and the more profound the sense of simply being. Equanimity arises with all that passes through, but cannot sully, this shining awareness.

So the Loving Kindness meditation has a multi-level skillfulness in its preparation for deeper practice. It cultivates considerable concentration by making the objects for concentration as concrete as words and as palpable as the gross movements of the breath as it enters and leaves the body. It mimics, in the superficial mind, the nature of the deep heart.

In the beginning we attempt to cultivate loving kindness. Later, loving kindness cultivates us. Cultivating loving kindness is also a means of softening the path as we progress. It allows, in the course of deepening awareness, material which has been suppressed to arise into an open-hearted consciousness. As mindfulness practice evolves from this concentrated presence, much of what has remained unconscious comes into consciousness. And we can use all the help we can get to remain open to that which we had closed off. But when loving kindness is the space into which the unloving arises, we do not meet the moment in fear but instead with fascination and gratitude and even joy for this sometimes difficult healing. Loving kindness is the perfect preparation for the battle. Later it will be seen that this battle was between aspects of one thing and that this "one thing" will lead you to a peace beyond just understanding.

In the concentration that is developed on the words and the breath in Loving Kindness meditation, we prepare ourselves for deeper practice. This is a broadening practice which widens the foundation on which all future practice will be built.

As one learns next the Loving Kindness meditation, we move to the Soft-Belly meditation. We take the practice of loving kindness into the body and out into the world. Returning again and again to soft belly, one feels the practice ride on a mindfulness of breath in the belly. Thoughts float through, feelings float through. Even a sense of someone meditating becomes just another bubble floating in the vast spaciousness of soft belly, merciful belly, open belly. And loving kindness fills the body and mind, meeting in the breath. Floating moment to moment in the spaciousness of being. The vastness just around the corner.

Mindfulness practice then takes the relationship with the breath and the concentration generated and begins to focus on the moment-to-moment unfolding of the sensations accompanying each inhalation, each exhalation. Against this wordless backdrop of sensation even the least moment of thought, the first whisper or word, the first flickering image, is seen instantly. All that is other than breath is noticed in its inception. Long before most thoughts are recognized thinking themselves, mindfulness meets them at the door through which they enter, and bows. It invites in even the uninvited, releasing all resistance or any attempt at control in order to explore thoughts' inner nature. To see them as they are. Spontaneous. Impermanent. Empty. Painful, if grasped.

Mindfulness of breath evolves into a focus on the content passing through—a moment of thought, a moment of fear, a moment of wondering, a moment of physical discomfort, a moment of pride, a moment of disappointment, a moment of joy. And the content of consciousness is experienced in a whole new way by watching how thoughts end. How every mind-moment has a beginning and a middle and an end, quicker than a flash of lightning. The lightning within lightning. Constant change unfolding. The mind dissolving moment to moment.

As we observe this flow of impermanence *the process* becomes quite evident. A moment of feeling dissolving into a moment of thinking, dissolving into a moment of hearing, dissolving into memory, dissolving into another feeling—increments in a process unfolding all by itself. An astoundingly impersonal flow of impermanence propelled by previous impermanent moments.

So first, it is content we notice and then process—a very healing and gratifying recognition. In seeing one's life, and life itself, as passing states of mind, the heart is free to seek "the appropriate," the intuitive moment, rather than select from long-conditioned content how to respond to a world of confusion and pain.

When process then becomes the focus and is explored we begin to note the space in which it floats. And this spaciousness becomes the context for deeper healing. Then whatever content arises, however process unfolds, it is seen floating in the spaciousness of pure awareness, the vastness of being so much greater than the fragments floating through.

As mindfulness deepens, we may encounter previously

numbed and rejected parts of our emotional life as anxiety in the mind or a hardness in the belly. We greet our rusted armoring. Though cognizant of its passing nature, some of this difficult material may present itself with considerable force. As it calls out for healing, we see the work that needs be done to confront these hindrances and clear the path for further progress.

It is at this point that such meditations as the Opening the Heart of the Womb meditation, the Forgiveness meditation, the Grief meditations and perhaps even the Eating meditation, become useful healing technologies to incorporate into our daily practice.

Although mindfulness and loving kindness may be a life's practice, in the course of this life certain qualities may require more immediate attention. For such circumstances the Heavy State meditation, the Pain meditation, the Healing meditation, and the Resistance meditation, are offered. These may be adjunct practices used in times of physical or mental discomfort or when practice is resisted and overwhelmed by rationality or doubt.

Progress in practice may be recognized watching the changing nature of our ordinary grief. At first, we may refer to it as "my suffering," but as participation in our life deepens, investigating the nature of the mind, the passing thoughts and feelings we always took so personally, so judgementally, are seen as arising spontaneously from process unfolding. And we see it is not *our* mind that so dismays us, it is *the* mind. That it is not *our* suffering but *the* suffering. The heart emerges from the separate to join in the universal. And we discover that it is our long-conditioned resistance to *the* pain which creates *our* suffering.

I've seen this progression in people who have come to these meditations for healing. At first they employ these techniques to heal "*my* body." The practice may initially be undertaken from a place of separation in the midst of lonely pain and perhaps helplessness. As the mind becomes concentrated, however, and the heart enters deeper those qualities which call for healing, the sense of separateness falls away and we see a profound entering into "*the* body"— a participation in the universal aspect of being and healing. It is no longer *my* cancer but *the* cancer, the cancer we all share. It is the lineage of healing in which each person finds him- or herself not at all alone but at one with tens of thousands in this same predicament, in this same body.

And yet the greatest healing awaits. It comes when we won't settle for just curing the body but demand entrance into *the* truth.

At this point we seek to go beyond even the universal, beyond *the* body to the *Real* Body, the body of being, the unseparate and inseparable, unborn, deathless body of pure awareness. This is the healing we took birth for. To heal from *my* body to *the* body to the *Real* Body, the body of awareness by which all else is known. Indeed, the *Real* Body, our true nature, is what we have been looking for our whole lives.

The final meditations included here are for approaching dying and moving beyond death. They provide an opportunity to enter directly that enormity of energy and light released when the formless bursts into form and when it recedes back into the vastness. Another opportunity to be fully alive, to go beyond even the Wheel of Birth and Death to the space in which it turns. To dissolve into the whorl of energy from which our light is emitted.

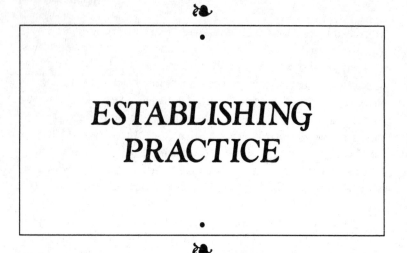

ESTABLISHING PRACTICE

Meditation is a means to an endlessness. It allows us to directly experience our true nature—the ever-healed, the unconditioned, the deathless. From that unimaginable vastness and clarity comes the peace and wisdom that we so long for. The space to accept ourselves "as is" and recognize our enormous power for healing, which is our birthright.

Many practices, including some of the "obstacle movers" offered in these meditations, allow a deeper penetration capable of uncovering blockages on the path to our liberation. These blockages are acknowledged and drawn deeply into the heart of a merciful awareness. But meditation stops nowhere, knowing that anyplace we "settle for" or momentarily place our feet is too impermanent and fragile to support our weight.

Meditation enters the mind to heal the mind, but

continues to those levels so deep and universal, only the word "heart" will suffice as description.

Meditation allows us to directly participate in our lives instead of living life as an afterthought.

To deepen awareness is to awaken. To awaken is to maintain "a continuity of the heart." To meet whatever comes, not only the confusing conditioning of the mind, but the spacious unconditional presence that lies beyond. Meditation is not a denial of anything, neither this tangled, oft-conflicting conditioning nor the ever-healed that exists just over the horizon. It is an entering directly into consciousness with mercy and clarity. It is a deep seeing of what turns pain to suffering. And how we cling to that suffering rather than let go into the vast unknown. Into the freedom inherent in our true nature. So we explore the mind, not to master it so much as to not be mastered by it. We are not making war on the mind, we are making peace with it.

Although we have spoken for years about the value of a daily meditation practice because of the riches it has brought into our life, for many committed to the "long haul" I suspect the term *regular practice* is more skillful. Indeed, a highly respected meditation teacher recently mentioned that even with his long established practice it was often hard to maintain a daily sitting outside the retreats he taught so regularly. Imagined priorities overwhelm the mind in a sense of "something more important to do." Big surprise, the mind has a mind of its own! And there is nothing like a regular practice to display this in a very healing manner.

We do the best we can. It is more important to have a continued sense of confidence and willingness to investigate the present in a continuous application of awareness to the vagaries of the mind/body, than to get stuck in some idea of who we *should* be and how we *should* practice.

In a desire to free ourselves we need be mindful of the tendencies toward judgment (it's the nature of *trying*) which arise in the course of any attempt to accomplish a task. The more we wish to have quiet sittings, the less quiet our sittings may feel. That wishing, that longing for things to be otherwise, creates an agitation. But in meditation nothing is eluded or discarded, and we don't attempt to "get around" this resistance or agitation, but rather focus directly on it. Indeed, the object of our focus is not of such consequence as the quality of that focusing, the quality of attention that is brought to the moment. We could become "lightened" by watching anger or fear as quickly as watching any other state of mind. For it is not the contents of the mind, but the quality of awareness that approaches these·qualities of mind that heals and frees. Our job is not to become a saint, but to become a whole human being.

Don't become stuck in ideas of how to practice. Just practice. Even if such ideas seem to come from the book in your hand at this moment, trust your own process. Cultivate an ongoing relationship to the mind, a continuity of awareness, which regularly allows you to trust the ground beneath your feet to indicate the next step to be taken.

Each time we focus awareness we condition the next moment toward clarity. We learn to navigate by the heart. As the old mind of old concepts and patterns dissolve into the process, pained voices recede into the background and we act from the appropriate, from the moment, not from old, often unsuccessful, ways of becoming. All that we seek is present in that sense of presence by which we know we are alive. It is from that joy of simply being that healing arises in the mind and brings us home to the heart of understanding.

As the God-drunken poet Kabir points out, for the person "who has heard the flute," the song of our true heart, who has lived a moment in their Real Body, the body of pure awareness, there is no question. Only an openness, a great "don't know" by which to navigate past our tiny knowings into the immensity of being. The space all these knowings bob in. The vast awareness in which these objects of awareness float and are healed.

When our teacher, Neem Karoli Baba, was asked how to raise profound spiritual awareness, he said, "Just love everybody." To establish practice is to cultivate mercy and awareness in yourself for the benefit of all sentient beings.

These techniques are for "tending one's garden." Each is a gardening implement.

At first when we approach the unexplored mind, it is like a stretch of wild, untended ground. All that grows there arises uninvited from passing happenstance and previous conditions. In some areas weeds choke out flowers. In others the ground is barren and impervious to life. Here and there seeds remain ungerminated. All about is deadfall obscuring the rich soil beneath. While just under the surface old roots, so slow to disintegrate, leave little room for new growth.

Some of the meditative tools offered in this book are used in the garden to break the hard surface, such as the Loving Kindness meditation and the Soft-Belly practices. Others are for refining the soil, such as the Forgiveness meditation and the Mother of Mercy meditation. Some are for turning the soil and digging deeper, such as the Mindfulness practice and the Body Exploration meditations, which are continually employed to recondition the ground and weed the garden. A few are used to encourage germination and to mulch tender shoots such as the Resistance, Grief, and Eating meditations. All can be useful to help us through "the narrow places" on the path through the garden. Each in its own way cultivates the conditions in which the wild flowers of grace can flourish.

Because this garden has gone so long untended much has occurred to limit growth. These limitations, these hindrances to further germination, need be addressed directly. Many of these are "obstacle-moving practices" for removing boulders or pulling stumps to make further use of this fertile soil. Many of these practices such as the Heavy State (afflictive emotion) meditation, the Heart of the Womb meditation, the Pain meditations, or the Healing meditations are specialized tools for removing specific obstacles. Each is appropriate for some aspect of the preparation, planting, and harvesting of the remarkable blossoms which arise spontaneously in the process of our liberation. This process begun in the heart expands into the mind/body and comes full-circle back to the heart. Each meditation has the potential for clearing another stratum of obstruction between the heart and the mind.

Mindfulness and Loving Kindness are foundation practices which are as sun and water to the garden. Regular application intensifies growth and deepens the roots of the heart.

One begins in the heart to soften the way for the mind and body to be experienced wholeheartedly without judgment or fear. As we open the heart, certain obstacles may become evident in the pain in the mind or body. Specific meditations are offered to approach each with the healing wisdom and awareness which mercifully receives the moment in a new softness and appreciation. And the process continues effortlessly. Referring to this effortless unfolding in Zen, they say, "Spring comes and the grass grows by itself."

It is often slow going at the beginning because concentration is still increasing and may yet take a while to develop. But liberation is a process and each step is so precious. Indeed, in the beginning with such meditations, by oneself or even with a capable teacher, there may be difficulties. In large groups after one of these guided meditations, it is not uncommon for someone to share extraordinary openings. Others sit by somewhat glumly thinking,

"How come nothing happened for me? What a dud I am! Everyone's going to get enlightened but me," but it is often those who think they didn't quite "get it" who later display considerable insight into that which obstructs their happiness. They may well have seen the nature of that which limits awareness or forgiveness or mercy or letting go, more clearly than one who in a "lucky moment" was momentarily able to get beyond the qualities they were examining. It is often when it "doesn't work" that the work to be done is most clearly defined.

Make these meditations your own. Experiment! Find the language and phrasing that is appropriate for you. Trust your own great genius for healing. Let the heart choose what is suitable in these meditations. One may be drawn to only one or two of those suggestions. Work with those that "feel right," not the ones you think you "should." Let the heart be the healer of the mind and body. Let these meditations become your own.

Our foundation practice for the past thirty years has been the Mindfulness and Loving Kindness meditations. But there have also been periods when an adjunct practice deepened Ondrea's and my ability to apply what had been discovered in meditation. Healing and Pain practices have been a part of our particular karma and have been practiced on occasion very intensely for extended periods with considerable success.

As with any meditation or healing technique, it is not so much that one practice is better than another as that some practices are more suitable for one temperament or another. Indeed it is not the practice which liberates, but the intention, the motivation, the heartful effort with which it is applied. Even in a practice such as Mindfulness, whose basis is the development of a choiceless, merciful awareness, a subtle smugness or judgmentalness can develop from a false sense of control which slows the healing. So, too, if body sweeping practices are not done in the spirit of discovery, but instead are performed because of a "need to overcome," there may be additional difficulty. Each practice has the potential of becoming a trap if we do not use it as a means of deepening compassion and lessening judgement.

The more any practice is done because of a sense that it "should" be, the more self (sense of separation, fear, isolation) it will create. The more self, the greater the sufferer. Indeed, there are practices that focus on pain, which, unskillfully done, can create more of a holy war in the mind and body, an attempt to slay pain which leads to just more suffering. Practicing, for instance, the Pain meditation, at times we work for perhaps fifteen minutes at the very center of discomfort, but then take a break and just ride the breath like a surfer on a perfect wave.

It is all such a balancing act. Words such as "letting go" or "surrender" can be easily misleading, misinterpreted by old mind. Such ideas need be balanced with a sense of the appropriate.

So each technique needs to be done with balance and heart for the practice to take one beyond the method itself. For one not to be only a meditator but to become the meditation itself. Healing is a high-wire act, a balancing of energy with effort, or concentration with receptivity, of wisdom with compassion, of awareness with mercy, of insight with letting go, of appearances with that which lies beyond appearance. And the balancing of what we call birth with that which we refer to as death, and of all that precedes and exceeds each.

It may be that you only work with a few of these practices in the beginning and it is months or years before you are called back to do others. Trust that "still small voice within" by which the heart informs the mind of what the next step might be.

Having repeatedly used these meditations until you know them "by heart," you may sense their usefulness to another. Thus, the Healing meditations, Pain meditations, Heavy State meditations, and Dying meditations (as well as most of the practices in this book) may be of particular use to a patient or loved one. Because the work we do on ourselves is quite literally for the benefit of all sentient beings. We become a bit more spacious. We become a teaching in healing and letting go. But it should be noted that many people who have issues around control (it's never someone else, it's always just another part of ourselves) may not appreciate "being guided." Remember when offering such tools that some states of mind are resistant even to the best of intentions. For some it is their dignity to go it alone. Don't even be a healer. Just be merciful. Timeliness is a very important factor in the offering of these practices to another or to yourself.

Let your flower open but hold nowhere to the fruit. Let the seeds fall to the ground and germinate in your own great nature.

Treasure yourself.

These insights and ongoing processes are offered for the benefit of all who are drawn to looking inward.

Because we are not enlightened, though we have been lightened considerably by our practice, we are still very much in the same process as anyone reading this book. We are all playing our edge. We are all approaching the unexplored where real growth occurs.

The object is simply to become more aware, to have more life to live in each moment, to be fully alive.

More important than becoming a good meditator is being meditative. Looking inward toward the truth and the truth beneath that as well. Stopping nowhere, continuing the investigation. Living a moment at a time, a minute at a time, an hour at a time, a day at a time, a life at a time.

When meditation is no longer an exercise in the mind that lasts a few moments and instead becomes an uncovering of the heart, which suffuses even our dullest day, we have made the meditation our own. When wisdom supports mercy, we have become the meditation.

Trust the process.

THE USE OF GUIDED MEDITATIONS

G uided meditations are on-the-job training. Having been repeated many times, they internalize and become one's own. Then the guidance is not from these pages, but from the heart of direct experience.

Read these meditations silently to yourself or slowly to a friend. Or record them in your own voice, allowing the words to ride the breath, allowing space between each line of guidance. Most of these meditations, though they only occupy a few typeset pages, are meant to be practiced for about thirty minutes each. Recorded on tape for yourself or a friend, these guided meditations allow you to see from within the nature of that which clouds the mind as well as the nature of that which dispells and heals that density.

Because it is the intent of these practices to be repeated many times, certain insights are "programmed" into the meditation process to encourage and deepen wisdom. As one "works" with these insights they become integrated into the heart in a manner that is very healing.

On first using these meditations, in the course of developing them in your heart, if you find that the mind sticks on certain lines—that some concept or idea has caused a kind of reactive thinking—just notice any "business" you have with these ideas, and later reflect on these lines. Work with them during the day. Use these ideas, which have attracted thought, as a contemplation. Enter them directly to see what might be useful therein. Exploring them as a teaching, the meditation never stops. And your day becomes quite beautiful.

There are three levels of use to each of these practices.

The first is to read them to oneself as though the heart were speaking to the mind as just "good advice." As one begins working with these techniques, perhaps reading them aloud, one finds their feet on the path of healing. These readings familiarize the mind with the process and encourage the heart to participate.

The second way these practices can be used is as an object of contemplation. Using these practices at the contemplative level, one deepens a sense of their applicability. Such contemplations increase confidence in one's capacity to work with even the darkness and shadow of afflictive emotions that sometimes block the light of our true nature. This reflection in contemplation also has the ability to "work" with an insight and turn it into a "breakthrough" by reflecting on its meaning in our lives. It is an act of regarding steadily, with considerable concentration, that which is before the mind to bring it into the heart. It is this capacity for deep reflection which aids us to find *our* way on *the* Way.

The third means in which these guided meditations can be useful is as a meditation to enter consciousness directly, to see clearly what is *as it is*. This is the most profound of the three levels offered in each meditation. To enter directly the mind and to heal toward the heart. To go beyond the known and the "knower" to the truth which permeates all things.

The difference between meditation and contemplation is that meditation allows a direct entering into the process out of which insight and truth arises, while contemplation uses the insight of oneself or another as a means of extrapolating the truth.

Thus these practices can be used in three different ways. Read aloud to oneself or another as one might an operation manual for the mind or a love poem, the words riding on the breath, clearing the way for a deeper practice. Second, as a contemplation and internalization of the practice. And third, as an examination from within of the nature of being. Each level brings one closer to the truth. Each deepens the riches available. Ultimately, this process will insist one surrender into the very center of the heart of experience and simply be. It is as guided meditation, the third level of entrance into experience, that these meditations produce the deepest healing. One approaches the truth slowly, steadily, until the seeker and the sought disappear into the seeking itself. And the seeking disappears into that vastness, which for lack of a larger term, we call God.

The first informs the mind. The second reflects on that mind. The third goes beyond mind to the heart of the matter.

AN EXPLORATION OF THE HEART

The practice of exploring the mind and that which lies beyond begins and ends with the heart.

The first step in our liberation is the cultivation of the heart's natural compassion. Meditation begins with the practice of non-injury, a deep willingness to end the suffering in the world and in ourselves. In truth it may be impossible to be alive in a body without causing pain to other beings and species, but our *intention* can be to create as little pain as possible and to use this life for the benefit of others. Non-injury is an intention, a guideline for the mind from the nature of the heart.

We eat. We love in confused manners. We trip and fall over states of mind. And we learn the art of balance. To support the changes the heart suggests without becoming aggressive toward the mind. We are learning to live in a sacred manner.

What is called for is neither force nor acquiescence, but an active participation in the moment. It is an opening to let in healing. When Mahatma Gandhi was asked about the "passive resistance" he was teaching all over India, he replied, "There is nothing passive in my resistance. It is just non-violent." Gandhi's "non-violence" is a skillful means toward a peaceful mind and world. Violence originates from the mind. Healing from the heart.

So the heart and its "still small voice within" is taken as teacher on the path of liberation. And non-injury is its most obvious quality. Non-injury ranges from self-forgiveness to the end of world hunger. When we begin to practice non-injury, the judging mind, which gets so exasperated with our "trying" is not allowed its abusiveness without a deep response from a merciful awareness. Non-injury means to treat others—and ourselves—as the subject of our heart instead of an object in our mind.

This is not the judgement-inducing dictum of the Ten Commandments. This is a commitment to healing and purification—a will toward clear action. As with Buddhist precepts—such as non-killing, non-stealing, non-lying, non-sexual misconduct—non-injury and compassion are not divine rules carved in stone, but simply reflections in the mind of the nature of the heart used to reinforce stability and balance on the path. They are gentle reminders, teaching guides, along the shining path between what seem at times glaring opposites.

This is not the self-hating morality which turns *the* pain to *my* pain. It is rather "a sense of the appropriate" which rises naturally from levels of awareness deeper than our masks and posturings, deeper than the personality, or even the acquired self. Entering directly our essential being— the heart of the matter—our "natural goodness" is manifest unceasingly. Clear action clears the way for clearer actions. Kindness calms the mind.

AN INTRODUCTION TO LOVING KINDNESS

To clear the way, we relate to the mind from the heart. On the conceptual level, the namemaker, the images mind substitutes for the living, vibrating present—the "me-dreamer"—is mercifully observed.

Loving kindness meditation works with that level of thought—of name and form, of duality, of "I" and "other"—as a means of healing long-conditioned separation into the unconditional oneness of being. Loving kindness meditation concentrates healing on a level of mind that usually numbs the heart. Indeed our work is not so much to open the heart—which like the sun is always shining, but whose light is often obscured—but to open the mind so that the deep light of the essence of mind we call the heart can shine through.

By cultivating loving kindness in that aspect of mind that usually lives life as an afterthought, we change the context of our existence. We begin to live directly. We awaken.

This meditation uses the conceptual, word-oriented mindscape in perhaps its most skillful manner. It turns a hindrance into an ally.

The difference between receiving thought in a merciful awareness and being lost in thinking is the difference between liberation and bondage. Loving kindness deepens the responsive while softening the reactive.

Loving kindness is not unique in its ability to be cultivated. We can cultivate any mental quality. Most of us have intensified our fear and anger by holding so often to the contents of the mind as being all we are. Practice indeed perfects, and we have perfected our fear to a frightening degree. Practicing envy or anger cultivates the re-arising of indignation and resentment. Practicing loving kindness encourages the recurrence of mercy and awareness and the letting go of the hindrances to the heart—the self-interest, the fear, the separatism, the judgement, which limit our direct participation in the mystery.

In the acquired mind there floats a thought-bubble called "me" and a thought-bubble called "you," but in reality there is just a hum of being, a suchness. And we think we can judge the difference. But thinking is like that! To the judging mind, to the unloving prosecutor, all, including ourselves, is "other," and to the degree it judges the other it will judge itself. Herein lies the healing genius of Jesus' statement, "Judge not lest you be judged."

Mercy is the opposite of judgement. It is a heartful opening rather than a mindless closing. It affirms a sense of the appropriate. Mercy is the essence of responsibility, a broad firmament from which to respond as opposed to the narrow ledge of life-limiting reaction. To re-act is to act out, again and again, our inner pain with the same old suffering. Mercy unites; judgement separates. Mercy is the voice of the unitive, of our "natural goodness." Judgement is the cold wind in the abyss between the heart and the mind. Mercy does not judge its own absence. It is open even to our closedness. Judgement regards everything with an equal mercilessness. Judgement wounds; mercy heals.

Mercy is defined by some as pity, but pity is born of fear—it wishes not to experience the pain of another or of oneself. When we touch pain with fear, that is pity. When we fear our own pain, that is self-pity. But when we touch pain with love—that is mercy. Mercy is a blessing. Pity is a hindrance.

We learn to be loving by watching how unloving we are. Recognizing the painful characteristics of fear and anger, and experiencing the unbearable closedness in the mind and body, we observe how our natural spaciousness is obscured. Investigating areas of resentment and guilt and that place of separation from others and our deepest self, we sense the "rightness" of the practice.

We begin the meditation by sending care for our own well-being directly to ourselves using such words as "May I be happy," "May I be free of suffering." At first the words may seem rather mechanical, just words. These words may at first be met by a long-established mercilessness by feelings of not-enoughness and unworthiness: "Oh this is so self-indulgent, what a cop-out!" When we first attempt to bring love to ourselves, the idea that we don't deserve it often becomes quite noticeable. The ordinary grief may come up with various arguments to dissuade us from going deeper. Fear distracts the investigation, the letting go, the healing peace. These arguments arise from conditionings most precious to watch. They alert us to much of what is blinding us to the perfection, to the scintillation of this moment. It is attachment to such dense arisings that dulls us to our own beauty and attempts to convince us we're not worthy. That we are incapable of "lightenment." That we are fractured beings who are going to stay that way forever. These pained thoughts have been encouraged and repeatedly cultivated. Now we are cultivating something to displace this pain. We are allowing a much more fruitful form of consciousness than our negative distortions will admit. The nature of these positive qualities is such that they naturally replace less wholesome energies all by themselves.

A means of developing loving kindness toward oneself is to think of one's good qualities, to think kindly of oneself. We've worked with people who have said, "I have no good qualities. There is really not much that is lovable about me at all."

And we say, "That must be incredibly painful to feel like that, so unloved and unlovable."

"Yeh, it feels really awful not to be able to love anyone, even myself, even a little."

"There must be millions of people who feel like that."

"Those poor bastards. It is terrible for someone to feel like that. They're so lonely, so cut off."

"Wouldn't it be wonderful if we could help them."

"Oh God, yes. It's too much to bear! I wish someone could help them."

This incredible compassion for the human condition comes pouring through them. They talk so lovingly about their condition when it occurs in another and through it uncover a care for the unloved which was previously unnoticed under all the fearful self-negation. They now have recognized someone in need and that someone just turns out to be themselves. And they direct feelings of care and kindness to those parts of themselves that wish so to be whole. Buddha said, "You could look the whole world over and not find another being more deserving of love than yourself."

And this is exactly how the meditation is done. We focus a concentrated love on this being who is so deprived and so deserving of love. Then we radiate this loving energy, this concern for the well-being of others, out to all sentient beings everywhere.

When I first began doing this practice, if I found myself agitated in disagreement with someone, I would begin to send loving kindness not so much *to* them, as *at* them. I thought I would "cool them out," thinking "what a good meditator I am." But I was angry. It was really my own suffering I needed to confront. *I* was the one who needed the loving kindness. And in time, I learned that I had to generate love for myself first before I could open to another. To send loving kindness *at* another with whom I was angry was an ancient superiority trip which just created more separation. I wasn't doing them any favor. My action had the sour aftertaste of spiritual one-upmanship—using love and spirituality to suppress another and see them as inferior. Domination and game-playing. But as I made room in my heart for me, I gradually found the ability to relate to my anger and frustration without being threatened by it. And by accepting it as is, I could, at times, enter it with a merciful awareness capable of dissolving the glue of the pained self-image that holds our suffering together. And perhaps the other person too was allowed a bit more space to let go of their anger. To send love to another we must first be in our heart.

The power of loving kindness is so great that when we concentratedly project it out to others, they often can feel it. It is a subtle but tangible energy which can be consciously directed, like awareness in the heart, or the sun through a magnifying glass, to a shimmering point of light.

As the practice continues, moments of great openness are experienced and moments of considerable closedness. The irony of the opening heart is that the farther it opens, the farther it has to go to close. Thus when the opening heart closes, one feels as though they have never been so closed before. But the meditation practice continually seeks new and deeper levels of learning in order to keep the heart open—even open to the heart being closed. Able to touch the unloving with loving kindness. It is the healing within healing.

Many have said that they would like to be more loving. They complain that, if they are to be "completely honest," their hearts aren't open more than a few moments a day—and that is a good day already!

We are so merciless with ourselves. Any amount of love in this life of forgetfulness and violence is a miracle. Any amount of love in this world so calling for healing and peace is true grace. A few moments of peace, of loving kindness, is a triumph over fear and old limitations.

With all our imagined unworthiness and fear, with all our doubts and desires, it is hard to be loving all the time. But it is harder not to be loving.

As an example of the power of the heart to take us beyond the separativeness of the mind, we offer these meditation practices on loving kindness. It is a fundamental practice for opening to ourselves, to our loved ones, to this world of suffering and joy in which we live. It is a meditation which, if experimented with for fifteen minutes a day for a few weeks, has the potential for expanding our lives and broadening our sense of play in the fields of the spirit. Many have used it regularly for years.

Loving kindness allows one to draw the mind concentratedly into the heart. As the attention gradually gathers, the words softly repeated become synchronized with each inhalation and each exhalation. They begin to ride on the breath in a gentle perseverance that clears the path toward the heart.

As with all the meditations and practices offered, these words become one's own as one takes the process within. Loving kindness, like mindfulness meditation, is a foundation practice. A lifetime's work. A lifetime's play.

For an extended version of the Loving Kindness (Metta) meditation, see A Gradual Awakening.

A GUIDED LOVING KINDNESS MEDITATION

(To be read slowly to a friend or silently to oneself.)

*S*itting comfortably, allow the attention to come gradually to the breath.

The breath coming and going all by itself deep within the body.

Take a few moments to allow the attention to gather within the even rhythm of the breath.

Turning gently within, begin to direct, toward yourself, care for your own well-being.

Begin to look on yourself as though you were your only child. Have mercy on you.

Silently in the heart say, "May I be free from suffering. May I be at peace."

Just feel the breath breathing into the heart space as we relate to ourselves with kindness and care.

Allow the heart, silently, to whisper the words of mercy that heal, that open. "May I be free from suffering. May I be at peace."

Allow yourself to be healed.

Whispering to yourself, send wishes for your own well-being:

"May I be free from suffering. May I be at peace."

Repeat gently with each in-breath into the heart, "May I be free from suffering." With each out-breath, "May I be at peace."

With the next in-breath, "May I be free from suffering." With the following out-breath, "May I be at peace."

Repeat these words slowly and gently with each in-breath, with each out-breath. Not as a prayer but as the extending of a loving care to yourself.

Notice whatever limits this love, this mercy, this willingness to be whole, to be healed.

"May I be free from suffering. May I be at peace."

Continue with this rhythm, this deepening of merciful joy and loving kindness drawn in with each breath, expanding with each exhalation.

"May I be free from suffering. May I be at peace."

Let the breath continue naturally, as mercy for yourself, your only child, for this being within.

Though at first these may only feel like words echoing from the mind, gently continue. There can be no force here. Force closes the heart. Let the heart receive the mind in a new tenderness and mercy.

"May I be free from suffering. May I be at peace."

Each breath deepening the nurturing warmth of relating to oneself with loving kindness and compassion. Each exhalation deepening in peace, expanding into the spaciousness of being, developing the deep patience that does not wait for things to be otherwise but relates with loving kindness to things as they are.

"May I be free from suffering. May I be at peace."

Allow the healing in with each breath. Allow your true spacious nature.

Continue for a few breaths more this drawing in, this opening to, loving kindness. Relating to yourself with great tenderness, sending well-being into your mind and body, embrace yourself with these gentle words of healing.

Now gently bring to mind someone for whom you have a feeling of warmth and kindness. Perhaps a loved one or teacher or friend.

Picture this loved one in your heart. With each in-breath whisper to him or her, "May you be free from suffering. May you be at peace."

With each breath draw that loved one into your heart, "May you be free from suffering."

With each out-breath filling them with your loving kindness, "May you be at peace."

With the next inhalation drawing their heart closer to yours, "May you be free from suffering."

With the following out-breath extending to the loved one a wish for his well-being, "May you be at peace."

Continue to breathe the loved one into your heart, whispering silently to yourself, to them, "May you be free from suffering. May you be at peace."

Continue the gentle breath of connection, the gentle wish for their happiness and wholeness.

Let the breath be breathed naturally, softly, lovingly into the heart, coordinated with your words, with your concentrated feelings of loving kindness and care.

"May you be freed of any suffering. May you know the deepest levels of peace."

Send them your love, your compassion, your care.

Breathing them in and through your heart.

"May you be free from suffering. May you know your deepest joy, your greatest peace."

And as you sense them in your heart, sense this whole world that wishes so to be healed, to know its true nature, to be at peace.

Note to yourself, "Just as I wish to be happy so do all sentient beings."

And in your heart with each in-breath, with each out-breath, whisper, "May all beings be free of suffering. May all beings be at peace."

Let your loving kindness reach out to all beings as it did to your loved one, sensing all beings in need of healing, in need of the peace of their true nature.

"May all beings be at peace. May they be free of suffering."

"May all sentient beings, to the most recently born, be free of fear, free of pain. May all beings heal into their true nature. May all beings know the absolute joy of absolute being."

"May all beings everywhere be at peace. May all beings be free of suffering."

The whole planet like a bubble floating in the ocean of your heart.

Each breath drawing in the love that heals the world, that deepens the peace we all seek.

Each breath feeding the world with the mercy and compassion, the warmth and patience that quiets the mind and opens the heart.

"May all beings be free from suffering. May all beings be at peace."

Let the breath come softly. Let the breath go gently. Wishes of well-being and mercy, of care and loving kindness, extended to this world we all share.

"May all beings be free of suffering. May all beings dwell in the heart of healing. May all beings be at peace."

*There is a phantom
in this painful dream
of who we wish we were—
the imagined self.*

*Don't be fooled
by a thought
into believing (another thought)
you are less
than God.*

SOFT BELLY

We are conditioned to suffer. The society of the hard-bellied and deeply pained conforms to this lowest denominator. We wander hard and lost through our lives until we awaken with a deep sigh of letting go and soften to the path of mercy.

When growth has become the priority, soft belly becomes the context for our letting go. Observing the relative openness or closedness of the belly gives insight into when and how we are holding to our pain. When the belly is hard there is holding. Some degree of fighting or posturing is resisting and hardening to the moment, attempting to control. You may have to come back to soft belly dozens of times an hour.

The belly is an extraordinary diagnostic instrument. It displays the armoring of the heart as a tension in the belly. The deeper our relationship to the belly, the sooner we discover if we are holding in the mind or opening into the heart. Trying tightens the belly. Trying stimulates judgement. Hard belly is often judging belly. Even trying to understand what is being said now, the belly may tighten.

Don't try only to understand. Enter the process. In soft belly simply allow understanding to arise, all by itself, from your true nature.

Beyond the mind is everything you long, in the mind, to know. But the great irony of the spiritual search is that what we are looking for is *what is looking.*

It is difficult to see that which sees, but not impossible. It takes some work to let go of old ways of seeing. Softening the belly is a beginning.

Indeed we are programmed to hold to our pain, to turn it to suffering. We are taught to harden the belly, to hide its fullness, its roundness, its spaciousness. Women in particular are programmed to be "attractive." Encouraged to wear undergarments that compress the belly and decrease the sense of spaciousness. Men, too, can often be noticed "holding in the belly" to be acceptable. Implored to be hard-bellied by a culture which confuses hardness with beauty. It is a dangerous way to live if one wishes to be fully alive.

The more one thinks that he or she *is* the body, the tighter the belly will be at times. There are so many levels of letting go into the enormity of being, but when there is a holding in of the belly the heart is not so available.

Ondrea and I have been doing this practice for years. And still we notice again and again that the belly needs to be reminded that it has unconsciously tightened to that which we wish to remain unconscious of. So you inhale down into the belly. And you exhale out past the heart. And the belly softens and you find room in your body for healing, for being, for liberation. The softer the belly, the greater the capacity to stay present and awake during the dense dream of heavy mental states. Soft belly encourages investigation of the body-patterning that accompanies such states. It allows exploration without getting drawn into their familiar, seductive thought-patterns. We cannot over-estimate the importance of softening.

Some years ago Ondrea and I turned to each other and said, "You know, it's time for us to stop auditioning for the kids. We've got the job!" We are constantly auditioning for the people we want love from. Our parents, our children, our lovers, our co-workers, our mates. Hard belly is always auditioning, posturing, angling for control. But, this is it. You've got the job. You've taken incarnation. Now, deepen soft belly to make room in your life for your life.

・

A GUIDED SOFT-
BELLY MEDITATION

(To be read slowly to a friend or silently to oneself.)

Let your attention come into the body.
Let awareness come to the level of sensation in the body.
Feel the physical sensations of being in a body.
Sensations of the buttocks on the chair or on a pillow. The pull of gravity.
Sensations of the chest moving, the breath.
Sensations in the neck, the weight of the head.
Feel this body you sit in.
Gradually allow your attention to come to the belly.
And begin to soften the belly.
Make room for the breath in the belly.
Breathing in, belly rises.
Breathing out, belly falls.
Soften to receive the breath down into the belly.
Allow the breath to breathe itself in soft belly.
Each breath softening, opening, releasing.
Inhalation, belly rising, filling with softness.

37

Exhalation, belly falling, releasing any holding.
Expanding and contracting belly.
Soft belly.
The breath breathing itself in the softness.
Letting go in the belly. Levels and levels of softness.
So much grief held in the belly, so much fear and armoring.
Let it all float in soft belly.
Not hardening it to suffering. Just letting it be in mercy, in soft belly.
Notice how even a single thought can tense the belly, harden it to armoring, to separation, to grief.
Letting go with each inhalation, softening the belly.
Letting go with each exhalation, making space.
Each exhalation breathing out the pain. Letting it go.
Soft belly. Merciful belly.
Levels and levels of softening.
Levels and levels of letting go.
So much room for liberation. So much room to be in soft belly.
Have mercy on you. Each breath softening.
Softening the belly to uncover the heart.
Letting go in the belly of the old holding which blocks the heart.
Each exhalation letting go of the pain. Breathing out the hardness, the armoring. Making room for your life in soft belly.
Expectation, judgement, doubt. Old griefs congregate in the belly. Softening allows them to disperse, to dissolve in soft belly. Pains, fears, doubts dissolving, dissolving into the softness, the spaciousness of a merciful belly.
Let it all float in soft belly. Have mercy. Levels and levels of softening meeting the moment.
Levels and levels of being in soft belly.
Breathing in, breathing out in soft belly.
Even if hardness is discovered in the midst of the

increasing softness, just watch it float through. Let the hardness float in the softness. Nothing to change, no urgency in soft belly. Let urgency float in the softness. Room even for the pain in the mercy and awareness of soft belly.

Let the sound of these words pass right through you. Don't hold anywhere. Trust the process.

Let all that arises pass through the spaciousness of soft belly.

And let your eyes gently open.

And as your eyes open, notice at what point the belly tightens once again. At what point the "someoneness" reasserts itself and you feel a need to protect. At what point does the armoring reestablish its long presence?

Softening with the eyes wide open to the world.

Softening to the pain we all share and the legacy of healing exposed in the deepening softness.

SOFT-BELLY MINDFUL BREATHING MEDITATION

(To be read slowly to a friend or silently to oneself.)

When the belly has softened and opened to awareness, the breath within becomes quite noticeable. This contact with the breath is the next step. We have opened to mindfulness.

Let your attention settle into the body you sit in.

Allow it to come to the level of sensation in the body.

Not thinking about sensation, but feeling directly the multiple changing movements of sensation in the body.

Feel the pull of gravity. The hands as they touch. The feet as they contact the floor. Sensations of being in a body.

Awareness and sensation meeting moment to moment.

The flickerings of sensation. Vibratory pulsations, tinglings, sensations of pressure, of hardness or lightness, of hot or cold. The sensations of living in a body.

Notice the sensations in the chest generated by the process of breathing. Muscles expanding and contracting.

Notice how breathing creates sensation in various parts of the body.

Feel the breath as it enters at the nostrils. Examine any sensation noticeable in the throat as the breath passes through.

Feel the muscles of the chest expanding and contracting with each breath. Notice how the broad flat muscles of the back stretch and release with each inhalation and each exhalation.

Know the breath in the body fully.

Notice sensations at the abdomen, a filling and emptying with each breath.

Awareness of whole body breath.

Let the awareness come wholly to the belly.

Receive the sensations that accompany each breath as the belly rises with each inhalation. Notice the changing flow of sensation as the belly naturally drops with each exhalation.

Rising belly. Falling belly.

Breathing in, breathing out in soft belly. In spacious belly.

Let the belly soften to receive the whole breath.

When breathing in, note your breathing in. Notice the point at which the in-breath is released and exhaled. Know that you are breathing out.

Mindfulness of breathing at the belly.

Not thinking the breath, experience it directly as sensation floating in soft belly. In merciful belly.

Spacious belly.

Note the very beginning, middle, and end of each inhalation.

Notice the space between.

Recognize the beginning, the middle, the end of each inhalation. And the space between.

Recognize the very first moment of the breath as it begins to be drawn into spacious belly. A flow of constantly changing sensation accompanying each breath.

Soft belly.

Receptive belly.

Watching the breath breathe itself moment to moment.

Sensations flowing in softness.

Breathing in.

Breathing out.

So simple.

Awareness and sensation meeting moment to moment. Constantly changing with each breath.

No force.

If the mind wanders, bring it back gently to the sensations that accompany the breath in the belly.

Not controlling the breath, just receive it in clear awareness focused in the belly. If other sensations momentarily predominate—the pull of gravity on the body, a passing discomfort—just notice these sensations floating and return awareness wholly to the sensations of the breath breathing itself in soft belly.

Sensation arising and dissolving moment to moment in the flow of breath received in the belly.

Thinking arises uninvited. Watch it come. Watch it go. Nothing to hold to. Thoughts float like bubbles through the mind, arising and dissolving. Return gently to the sensations that accompany each inhalation, each exhalation.

Mindfulness of breathing in soft belly.

Awareness focusing to receive more and more of the subtle sensations that flicker within each arising, each falling of the belly.

Observing the sensations in soft belly that accompany each in-breath, each out-breath. Gently. Moment-to-

moment sensation. Moment-to-moment breath. Thought, feeling, floating in soft belly just inside the breath.

In soft belly there is room for it all.

Room to be born. Room to be healed.

And the breath breathes itself in the vastness.

TO TAKE A SACRED BREATH

The concept of the Holy Ghost is based upon the idea of the sacred breath (the original Greek translation). It is breath that connects the heavy, outer body with the inner, light body. (See the Dying meditation.) An object brushing the nerves of the heavy body is received by the body of awareness, the light body within, as sensation. Breath allows the body of awareness to remain in our birth body. It maintains and sustains its perfect cradling within. When the breath stops, that connection is broken and the light body floats free, as the heavy body crumples into gravity. The breath is as sacred as life.

Usually there is so little trust in life, in the next moment, that the breath is somewhat held. Fear tends ever so subtly to shape the breath. It holds here, it pushes there. We limit breath's deep entrance holding shallow to the mind. We seldom take a "natural breath."

A friend, who had been meditating for some time, found in her practice a period of difficulty which seemed to get more intense as she tried assiduously to uproot it. She saw directly how her resistance to these uncomfortable, afflictive mental states were encouraging them to stay. Negative attachment. So, as she tells it, she walked for hours "just to get one 'natural breath.' " For some time she walked mindfully back and forth across her room until the mind sank into the heart. And beyond even her mindfulness, indeed beyond the mind, the heart arose in the breath that breathed itself spontaneously through her body. Her mind settled and the pain in her legs and chest diminished. It was a moment of deep healing when, for an instant, the inner and outer were wholly in balance, directly connected, with no "mental middleman" thinking that the breath or the body were separate from the sacred.

When the breath breathes itself without self-consciousness or guile, the connection between the outer body and the inner awareness, between the mind and the heart, is wholly unimpeded. The natural tides of the breath float in the sacred vastness. The breather dies into the breath. There is no longer even the idea of breath but just the flow of being unfolding. Only breathing; breathing itself. All nouns vanish into a single verb: being—endless suchness.

And though being is self-existent, our experiences of that spaciousness are dependent on various mental qualities which are constantly in flux. Tuning to the breath, we enter the body of awareness within our flesh and bones.

A single sacred breath can clear the body and mind of its momentary graspings.

To take a sacred breath is to allow the suchness of being (that we may label God, but never cease to explore) spontaneously and wordlessly to enter consciousness.

In the great sigh of letting go the belly opens and we take a sacred breath.

FORGIVENESS

The beginning of the path of liberation is the end of life unlived. It is a finishing of unfinished business. To finish business means an end of relationships as business, not a totaling of accounts. It is not a waiting for others' acceptance or forgiveness. It is an acceptance of them and ourselves, as is—even if that "as is" includes their not accepting us. When we have touched another with true forgiveness we no longer require anything in return. Our business is done. Entering our lives as complete beginners, we take each breath as though it were the first; watching each thought as though it were the last. Becoming wholly alive.

One of the first steps on the path of liberation is the deepening of forgiveness. It is an expansion into the world of the inner workings of loving kindness. Forgiveness softens the path and eases continued progress. It is a letting go of the painful resentment that naturally arose between different desire systems. It is the deep resolution of conflict between individuals, as well as oppositional aspects of ourself.

Business is finished with another in the same way it is completed within. It is a meeting of the unhealed with a merciful healing, a profound forgiveness and letting go into the heart of the matter. It is a completion of what a dying musician called the "unfinished symphony." The dreams and longings just beneath the surface of our worldly persona. The unfulfilled, the uncompleted, the oft-resented inheritance of a life only partially lived.

Coming upon long unresolved issues and old holdings—feelings of being betrayed by the body, by friends, by the world—we find it difficult simply to let go. The resistance and holding around the unresolved, the unapproached, has contracted so that it seems to take considerable effort to loosen it back to its natural openness. But forgiveness can allow the yet-held to slip away lightly.

In theory it would be ideal to just let go of heavy states such as resentment or fear or guilt. But in practice we discover that the considerable momentum of our identification with such feelings has cultivated deep roots which are not so easily extirpated. Before we are fully able to "just be mindful" of such feelings, to let them float in a merciful awareness, without the least tendency to cling or condemn, it may be very helpful to consider the practice of forgiveness. It exemplifies the potential for letting go—an open-handed acceptance which offers mercy to the gavel-fisted judgement of the often unkind mind. An unexpected healing.

Forgiveness allows us to let go of some of our grief—the curtains of resentment and the fear which filters all but the shallow and desperate in the mind. Forgiveness lessens clinging and allows the agitated mind to sink a bit more deeply into the healing heart.

Cultivating forgiveness presents the possibility of freedom from the ancient incarcerations of the judging mind. Forgiveness allows anger to float in a merciful awareness. Like soft belly, it makes room for our lives. It is the natural expression of the unobstructed heart. It resolves separation and allows the mind to go beyond itself. Like loving kindness, it is a cultivation in the mind of the spaciousness of the heart. Practiced daily, forgiveness opens the mind to the heart's natural compassion.

When beginning the practice of the Forgiveness meditation, one first needs to recognize that guilt arises uninvited. It is important to use forgiveness not as a means of squashing guilt, or even outmaneuvering the unforgiveness of another, but as a means of dissolving obstructions. At first while contemplating a particular situation, you might feel strongly that you've done nothing wrong, "so why ask or send forgiveness?" But emotions are not so rational. Indeed it is irrational to expect emotions to be rational; they have a life of their own. We ask for forgiveness and offer forgiveness not only for some injury or wrongdoing, experienced or otherwise, but for our own well-being. We can stand no longer to carry the load of our long-held resentments and guilts.

But first, and of prime importance, is to investigate that which forgiveness heals. One does not attempt to *submerge* anger or fear with a forgiveness technique. To force forgiveness, to attempt to touch with forgiveness that which we can hardly approach with a clear awareness, does not further our efforts. The forgiveness technique is most potent when it is used at the appropriate time. First we need to be mindful and investigative of our anger, our distrust, our holding, before the enormous power of forgiveness can reach as deep as it is able. One does not use forgiveness *instead* of the investigative work on what closes the heart, but as an adjunct, an ally, to this healing.

If at first forgiveness feels a little awkward, please

remember that forgiveness is not a condoning of an unskillful action that has caused injury but a touching of the actor with mercy and loving kindness. We cannot condone murder, but we may in time be able to touch the murderer with some understanding, lessening our own fear, opening our lives a bit more. Forgiveness benefits oneself not just another. It touches, in ourselves with a new mercy and understanding, those same states of mind that we judge in another. The qualities we forgive in another are qualities we have long judged in ourselves. Forgiveness heals us back into our heart.

Although we may be opening our heart to another it is primarily a means of self-healing. Indeed, forgiveness may be felt across hundreds of miles and even acknowledged, but that is not the primary purpose of this meditation. In fact, to wait for such acknowledgment is an example of how we perpetuate unfinished business. To be awaiting anything is to cultivate a feeling of "unfinishedness." Forgiveness finishes business by letting go of the armoring that separates one heart from another. As one teacher said, "As long as there are two there is unfinished business. When the two become one, the heart whispers to itself in every direction."

In working with each of these meditations, our own natural wisdom recognizes yet other, deeper levels of our healing toward which they can be directed. They assist us in using our own great genius for healing, our homesickness for God, to guide us. Though forgiveness is quite powerful in the form it has most usually been practiced, we discover through the meditations yet another aspect of its healing: when patients we were working with began sending forgiveness directly into the center of their discomfort, they found a profound softening and opening ensuing.

Many who are ill feel betrayed by the body. And they banish the body from the heart. They exile their illness. Touching with forgiveness that which they had so often abandoned with condemnation and deep resentment, they allowed the gentle miracle of forgiveness to permeate their body/mind. They made the practice their own and began sending forgiveness into their tumors, their degenerative heart disease, their AIDS, and discovered peace where before there had been war. Relying on nothing of the past they entered profoundly into what was needed *as* it was needed. The ocean of awareness dissolved their footsteps behind them, leaving no trace but only the ground beneath their feet. In this very instant all that had been sought was found.

Our business is finished when we can receive a previous object of resentment with mercy and soft belly. Waiting for anything in return, even acceptance, even understanding, our business remains unfinished. But when we want nothing in return and accept people—ourselves included—as is, even though they don't accept us, then nothing separates our mind from our heart, or any others'.

Cultivating forgiveness softens the clingings of the mind and opens the holdings of the body. It personifies healing.

In the deepest stages of forgiveness one finds that there really is no "other" to send forgiveness toward but only a sense of shared being. We experience the one mind, the one heart, in which we all float.

Many years ago, during a very difficult time in my life, sitting very alone by a pond in a redwood forest, practicing the forgiveness meditation, the practitioner disappeared, and all became forgiveness: the trees were forgiveness, the boulders, the pond, the salamander crawling across my sneaker. The world became an all-accepting love. And in my mind a voice whispered that I was forgiven for everything I had ever done. To which the mind responded, "Yes, but . . . but that's not possible. There has been so much." To which the heart replied, "You are completely forgiven, it is all done. If you want to pick it up again that is up to you, but it is all yours from now on." How difficult it was to accept, to allow such an enormous kindness into my heart—and how liberating!

The beauty of the forgiveness meditation is that it cannot be done wrong. Be gentle with this process. Choose one who provokes only a little pain at first. No bravado! If forgiveness does not flow from the moment, certainly that which blocks forgiveness becomes more clearly defined. To know the blockages of the heart, to acknowledge them, to open to them, is precisely the healing that is needed. As one continues the practice of forgiveness, a new confidence arises. We increasingly sense the workability of so much we had hardened to out of fear and a profound sense of incompleteness within ourselves. Forgiveness is a practice which sometimes makes us think "nothing is too good to be true!" Forgiveness is a gift from the heart to the mind.

A GUIDED FORGIVENESS MEDITATION

(To be read slowly to a friend or silently to oneself.)

*B*egin to reflect for a moment on what the word "forgiveness" might mean. What is forgiveness? What might it mean to bring forgiveness into one's life, into one's mind?

Begin by slowly bringing into your mind the image of someone for whom you have some resentment. Gently allow a picture, a feeling, a sense of them, to gather there.

Now invite them into your heart just for this moment.

Notice whatever fear or anger may arise to limit or deny that entrance and soften gently all about it. No force; just an experiment in truth which invites this person in.

Silently, in your heart, say to this person, "I forgive you."

Open to a sense of their presence and say, "I forgive you for whatever pain you may have caused me in the past, intentionally or unintentionally, through your words, your thoughts, your actions. However you may have caused me pain in the past. I forgive you."

52

Feel for a moment that spaciousness of the heart which always contains the possibility of forgiveness.

Let go of those walls, those curtains of resentment, so that your heart may be free, so that your life may be lighter.

"I forgive you for whatever you may have done that caused me pain, intentionally or unintentionally, through your actions, through your words, even through your thoughts, through whatever you did, through whatever you didn't do. However the pain came to me through you, I forgive you. I forgive you."

It is so painful to put someone out of your heart. Let go of that pain. Let them be touched for this moment at least with the possibility of forgiveness.

"I forgive you. I forgive you."

Allow that person just to be there in the stillness, in the warmth and patience of the heart. Let them be forgiven. Let the distance between you dissolve in mercy and compassion.

Let it be so.

Now, having finished so much business, dissolved in forgiveness, allow that being to go on their way. Not pushing or pulling them from the heart, but simply letting them be on their own way, touched by a blessing and the possibility of your forgiveness.

Giving yourself whatever time is necessary, allow that person to depart, noticing any feelings as they leave.

Now gently bring into your mind the image, the sense, of someone who has resentment for you, someone whose heart is closed to you.

Invite them, just for this moment, into your heart. Notice whatever limits their entrance and soften all about that hardness. Let it float.

Mercifully invite them in and say, "I ask your forgiveness."

"I ask your forgiveness."

"I ask to be let back into your heart. That you forgive me for whatever I may have done in the past that caused you pain, intentionally or unintentionally, through my words, my actions, even through my thoughts."

"However I may have hurt or injured you, whatever confusion, whatever fear of mine caused you pain. I ask your forgiveness."

Allow yourself to be touched by their forgiveness. Allow yourself to be forgiven. Allow yourself back into their heart.

Have mercy on you. Have mercy on them. Allow them to forgive you.

Feel their forgiveness touch you. Receive it. Draw it into your heart.

"I ask your forgiveness for however I may have caused you pain in the past—through my anger, through my lust, through my fear, my ignorance, my forgetfulness, my blindness, my doubt, my confusion. However I may have caused you pain, I ask that you let me back into your heart. I ask your forgiveness."

Let it be. Allow yourself to be forgiven.

If the mind attempts to block forgiveness with merciless indictments, recriminations, judgements, just see the nature of the unkind mind state. See how merciless we are with ourselves. And let this unkind holding be softened by the warmth and patience of forgiveness.

Let it be so.

Feel their forgiveness now as it touches you.

If the mind pulls back, thinks it deserves to suffer, see this merciless mind. Let it sink into the heart. Allow yourself to be touched by the possibility of forgiveness.

Receive the forgiveness.

Let it be.

Gently bid that person adieu and with a blessing let them be on their way, having even for a millisecond shared the one heart beyond the confusion of seemingly separate minds.

Now gently turn to yourself in your own heart and say, "I forgive you," to you.

It is so painful to put ourselves out of our hearts.

Say, "I forgive you," to yourself.

Calling out to yourself in your heart, using your own first name, say "I forgive you."

If the mind interposes hard thoughts, that it is self-indulgent to forgive oneself, if it judges, if it persecutes you, just feel that density and let it soften at the edge. Just watch that unkind mind and let it be touched by forgiveness.

Allow yourself back into your heart. Allow you to be forgiven by you.

Let the world back into your heart. Allow yourself to be forgiven.

Let that forgiveness fill your whole body.

Feel the warmth and care that wishes your own well-being. See yourself as if you were your only child; let yourself be embraced by this mercy and kindness. Let yourself be loved. See your forgiveness forever awaiting your return to your heart.

How unkind we are to ourselves. How little mercy. Let it go.

Allow you to embrace yourself with forgiveness.

Let yourself be loved.

Let yourself be love.

And begin to share this miracle of forgiveness, of mercy and awareness. Let it extend out to all the people about you.

Let all be touched by the power of forgiveness, for all those beings who also have known such pain, who have so often put themselves and others out of their hearts, who have so often felt so isolated, so lost.

Encourage them with your forgiveness, with your mercy and loving kindness, that they too may be healed just as you wish to be.

Feel the heart we all share filled with forgiveness so that all might be whole.

Let the mercy keep radiating outward until it encompasses the whole world. Let the whole planet float like a bubble in your heart; the whole world bobbing on the ocean of infinite compassion.

May all sentient beings be freed of their suffering, of their anger, of their confusion, of their fear, of their doubt.

May all beings know the joy of their true nature.

May all beings be free from suffering.

Whole world floating in the heart. All beings freed of their suffering. All beings' hearts open, minds clear. All beings at peace.

May all beings, on every level of reality, on every plane of existence, seen and unseen, be freed of their suffering. May they all be at peace.

May we heal the world, touching it again and again with forgiveness. May we heal our hearts and the hearts of those we love by merging in forgiveness, by merging in peace.

WHOSE LIFE IS IT ANYHOW?

Who are you?

When you say, "I am," to what does that refer?

What is your true nature?

All that we have experienced in life has changed. Every thought, feeling, sensation, love making, doubt, argument, every breath has had a beginning, middle, and end. The body changes. The mind changes. All has been a fleeting momentary experience except one—the *"uh"* of being. The sense of presence by which we suspect we exist.

Look into your own experience. Look directly. Does *"uh"* have a beginning and an end? Or is it a sense of unending suchness, deathless, ageless?

Since the moment we became aware we were aware, there has been an underlying hum of being. Indescribable but directly experienceable.

Does *"uh"* take birth? Does it take death? Or is it the

ocean from which these waves are born? And into which each subsides?

This underlying sense of presence, this *"uh,"* is the only experience of a lifetime which has not changed. It is the space in which change floats.

When we investigate into what "I am" refers to, we search the "I" and discern constant becoming, an incessant grasping at someone, something, to be. Fear, old age, and death. Time. In the "I" nothing is real for long. But when we enter the "am-ness" there is just being. Not being *this* or being *that*. Not gain or loss. No triumphs and no despair. Am-ness is constant suchness. Or, as it is sometimes called, "a thus-ness"—the deathless, the unborn and undying essence of being. Even to call it *"uh"* is to verge on holy war. The drive to name the unnameable is our addiction to the mind, an aspect of the trembling "I" which longs for control.

Everyone's "I" is different. Everyone's am-ness is the same. There are dozens of "I"'s in each individual and billions of individuals. But there is only one am-ness. Indeed the experience of am-ness has been the same for all who have ever existed. Just *"uh."*

We believe we shall die because we have become convinced we were born. Take nothing secondhand. Explore for yourself this essential *"uh"* of being. Does it die? Was it produced from the birth of the body? Or was the body produced from it?

We believe we depend upon the body for our existence—but it is precisely the other way around. The body depends on us, the am-ness, our true nature, for its existence. And when the bright spark departs, the body becomes trash and a disposal problem.

It is a sacred recycling in which the container is discarded but the contents are returnable.

Where was our *"uh"* before we were born? What inhabits this flickering field of sensation we call "our body"? What is our Real Body, our unborn body? Our deathless body?

The born body is to the Real Body what a thought is to the mind. The Real Body is no body at all. It is the body of awareness.

It lights consciousness and inhabits all that we are conscious of.

It produces the *"uh"* of being. It is the only constant of a lifetime. In fact, it is the constant from which this momentary lifetime was created.

It is too large for heaven and religion makes it too small.

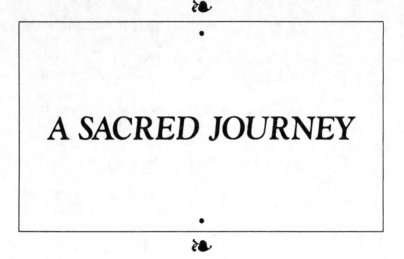

A SACRED JOURNEY

There is a sacred journey we were each born to undertake. It is the Great Healing.

We are explorers of the sacred unknown, of the truth that remains when all grasping at truth has subsided.

We are on a sacred pilgrimage that explores to our edge and beyond. Investigating the process and the space in which this process is floating. We are mapping the vibrating boundary between the known and the unknown. And we proceed, like Buddha or Madame Curie, past the fear at the gates, into the space beyond our knowing. We take step after step into unexplored territory where all growth occurs. Approaching the truth and healing that arise from the heart when we go beyond the mind.

We have taken birth into this scintillating, flickering body to discover the body in the body, the bright speck around which the pearl is formed.

Approaching this essence, we enter the breath within the breath, that to which Kabir referred when he spoke of God.

And it turns out that our true nature isn't even this spark that lights our body with consciousness, but the fire from which the spark was thrown. The formless "*uh*" of being not different than pure awareness.

We are born to explore our little body to find our true body. We are born to explore our little mind to find our true mind. We are born to explore our little heart to find our true heart. Our true heart, our true mind, is our Real Body.

There is a sacred exploration that awaits us all. It is a journey from here to now! It awaits in "just this much," this very instant, this millisecond of being. It is to discover what lies within. And within what? It is not to become Buddha or Jesus, it is to be the light to which each referred when he said "I."

ON USING THE NAME OF GOD

I am very comfortable using the word God because I don't have the foggiest idea what it means, but I see no place it is absent. And I can't deny that the word makes my heart sing.

Buddha, knowing the illusion of the superficial "I" and the verity of am-ness, nonetheless continued to use the word "I" as a convenience. In that same way, though I know there is no concept huge enough to contain our true nature, I use "God" as a convenience for the joy the truth emits. And if you follow "I" or "God" to its source the same will be discovered.

I do not sense God as some bribable paternalism in the sky, but rather the space in which such thoughts float. And the energy that allows that thought. Precisely the same energy that moves thoughts through the mind moves the stars across the sky. In the joy of God I feel more gratitude than any sense of possession or some special attention available from the "boss."

I often use the word "God" to express the unexpressible. But for many that word is tainted with abuse and old thinking. One can easily substitute the words "original nature" or just "nature." For some "Tao" or even "process" represents the mystery and the vastness.

In "God" is displayed the joy of being, our "natural goodness," and the celestial song of our great nature. It is a term of overwhelming delight. In "I" is the held and the lost, the self image, the pained and separate, the struggle, the confusion. Neither term is "real." "I" is not the truth; "God" is not the truth. The truth is the truth. Enter it directly. Go to the essence of each.

THE WAY
OF PRACTICE

In the beginning of spiritual practice, though I had read some about Buddhism, the Bhagavad-Gita was my daily companion and most of my quite informal meditations were heart practices from the Hindu tradition.

Soon I found teachers or, should I say, they found me, and I continued with these practices for some years.

This period of practice was very fulfilling and began to broaden the inner vision. And though this broadening was very healing, something in the heart was called to commit yet deeper. And once again, the practice found me.

An old poet friend, returning from three years as a Buddhist monk in Thailand, brought with him Mahasi Sayadaw's teachings on Vipassana, or mindfulness, practice. I sensed immediately that this more formal way of practice might be required if my mind was to sink into my heart at last. And though I recognized that old tendencies might use any technique as a control and posturing mechanism—behind which to hide my confusion and suffering—I sensed it could be applied deeply from the heart rather than superficially from the frightened, fragmented mind.

When I began the mindfulness practice, it seemed at first as though it was making me think more. But mindfulness is a focusing on the moment which reveals the machinations of the unexplored mind in a new light. Much to my chagrin, I was discovering how much my mind was mechanically engaged in thinking and fear cried out that perhaps meditation was going to make me crazy. But then the thought arose, "Well, considering how many foolish and unskillful things I've done in the past, with hotrodding, bar room brawls, drug addiction, and typical sexual confusions, how much harm could this meditation stuff really do me?!" So I made a deal with myself. I gave the practice three months. I figured if it only caused more difficulty I would know by then. Within six weeks the original contract with myself, to continue the experiment without judging it, had disappeared. The practice had established itself, teaching me to simply observe from the heart the ever-moving mind.

Of course my first question was what sitting posture I should adopt for long periods of meditation. Photos of yogis with legs winding around their necks were discouraging. But the practice itself recognized that the function of "finding one's posture" was simply to be able to sit the body down and maintain a stillness that necessitated very little extra attention. Sensing that all postures tend to arise from a place of posturing, I chose the simplest, easiest manner of sitting—a meditation bench.

When I began meditating using this kneeling bench, I found it was the best and most easily maintained position for extended practice. For years this posture worked perfectly for my needs. But over time my knees began to weaken and eventually I found that the practice of sitting with the knees bent under me on the floor was straining the joints and making the posture excessively discomforting. When I sat for long periods the knee-pain would become so severe and the difficulty in standing afterward so pronounced that I decided to change position.

There are two kinds of pain that arise from meditation. One disappears soon after standing. This is from a deep destressing and release that may at times be rather intense but fades when concentrated meditation ends. The other type is pain that sometimes develops when the body is strained by long periods of practice. Since the knees were being affected throughout the day by the morning sitting, I began to experiment with a zafu, a Zen meditation cushion, which required the legs to be folded in front of the body rather than under it.

This worked very well for years and I found much stability in what is called the "Burmese posture" where the legs are not pulled up on themselves but lie folded flat in front of one on the floor very comfortably.

But in the course of time the spinal difficulties encountered in my youth, for which I had undergone surgery when I was nineteen years old, began to strongly reassert themselves. Sitting for *any* period of time became a meditation on pain. Useful meditations indeed, but quite fatiguing.

During this period, my practice became irregular. And I focused more on the pain of those with whom we had almost daily contact in our work with the dying than solely on the attainment of a clear insight. It was more a meditation on compassion for the world of pain than it was a traditional mindfulness practice. Mindfulness, however, has a life of its own and once established tends to continue, no matter what other practices—or difficulties—are added to our spiritual life. Wishing to continue practice, I began meditating in a chair. Thus this deepening heartfulness aided clarity as well.

So after more than twenty years of practice I had to

abandon the zafu and sit in a chair.

Watching the adolescent mind, frightened to let go of its image of itself as a "yogi on a zafu," I felt like a dunce sitting in a chair. At times I would laugh aloud at how squeamish the mind was to go beyond its safe territory. "How can I practice non-attachment if I can't sit in the manner I am accustomed to!?" Meditation had apparently become a bit too safe. More a base camp than an exploratory focus on what lay beyond the next ridge. My change in posture had uncovered some subtle posturings accumulated within. It was time to die. To go beyond any idea of refuge as "a Buddhist" and enter the unfragmented spaciousness of the heart. To let go of becoming and simply be.

In a quiet place, when the heart is turned toward the truth, we *are* the Buddha. We are the lineage of self-inquiry and healing.

The new position in the chair, sitting with my hands folded in my lap and both feet flat on the floor, breathing quietly, watching as deeply as the moment allowed, became very satisfactory, indeed quite workable. And, because it expanded the meditation more and more into my daily life, it was also quite insightful. So natural was the posture it got so that I couldn't sit down in a chair without remembering my breath and the space it all floated in.

As meditation became integrated increasingly into the heart, a whole new level of practice evolved. More and more my daily life became my practice.

A year or two into the chair the degenerative spinal condition made sitting, for even five minutes, without constant readjustment of the body, impossible.

As conditions in the body changed, though the practice is always to meet the mind in a merciful awareness, the *way of practice* evolved. No longer sitting in a chair, I continued to meditate by lying on my side on the bed.

It was at this point, some years ago, that I began to refine and consistently apply the healing meditations we had been using with our friends and patients. Daily I sent a healing mercy and direct awareness into the area of discomfort. And the body responded with healing.

Now I can once again sit for extended periods in a chair. And even on a cushion for a while. But I have not abandoned what all this taught me and I continue to meditate on my side in bed as well. Noting whether I wake on the in-breath or out-breath and continuing deeper so each day is begun in the heart of clear awareness. And I am never "waiting to meditate."

What began so expectant and so large—exploring the nature of the universe—has become so small it only fits into "just this much."

CHOOSING A
TEACHER

It is more difficult to be a complete human being than a saint. It means nothing can be eluded or suppressed. It means taking on what Zorba called "the whole catastrophe."

When psychologists from Harvard went to India equipped with various psychological tests to evaluate the psyches of several highly developed spiritual adepts, they found that a few were "nearly certifiable." Much unfinished business had been "layered over" with powerful techniques and long-accumulated concentration. They had mastered the technology of their lineage, but they were not what one might call "whole human beings." They were skilled craftsmen with profound unresolved, and unintegrated, issues around their childhood, intimacy, control, power, sexuality, and fear. They were not the complete and effortless expression of the open heart or the clear mind.

As Krishnamurti put it, "The Saints were not total human beings. Most of them were rather neurotic. Their development was one-sided. Teach the young the art of listening and learning, and the art of observation. If you can do that, you've taught them everything."

Invited to be on a panel about the psychology of spirituality for three days with some of those same Harvard psychologists and His Holiness the Dalai Lama, I was touched again and again by the Dalai Lama's comment that "my only religion is kindness." Indeed, he said, "We can live without religion or meditation, but we cannot survive without human affection."

Because of the mind's tendency to project perfection on others, in the same way it projects imperfection on ourselves, we suggest that when choosing a teacher you retain a deep recognition that it is the *teaching* not the *teacher* that is to be venerated. To travel the path the heart is called to, and to know that as we mature in the spirit and "get the teaching" there are times when it is appropriate to leave that teacher, as did Buddha, and move on to the next teaching. But some teachers, subtly stuck in wanting students, use fantastic stories of deprivation and loaded terms like *sangha* or *satsang* to "keep their audience." As the Dalai Lama cautioned, "Beware of such teachers!"

Here and there you will hear a teacher who selectively quotes the Buddha as saying that "90 percent of practice was *sangha*" (the company of fellow travelers on the path). And indeed there is considerable value, at times, in being with others who too are struggling toward the surface. But 90 percent?!! I think not. All our work is done "alone" in the heart. Perhaps that teacher's desire for students, and our common wish for the perfect family, caused him to ever so subtly be attached to that particular statement. Good advice, but a bit exaggerated.

When we choose wisely a teaching, the teacher is appreciated but does not become an extension for our self-hatred and insecurity. I always like what Alexandra David-Neal said about her travels in Tibet during the early part of this century when she saw that teachers were chosen for their wisdom, not their personality or their parlor tricks. She said that if a particular teacher were drunk 40 percent of the time the students just figured that was the teacher's problem, and only practiced with him the other 60 percent of the time. They chose a teaching wisely and a teacher with considerable discriminating wisdom.

My teachers have been an indispensable part of my growth, but a few, at least one, gave advice that was not appropriate to my path. Fundamentalist inclinations, fear of relationships, spiritual rivalries, and personal needs occasionally clouded their otherwise clear eyes. To each I give my profound appreciation and continue, like God's fool, on the path with a heart.

When choosing a teacher, just remember the hard work that is to be done and get on with it. In the Southern Buddhist tradition in which I practiced for many years, the word "guru" is not used, but instead a term which means "spiritual friend." A spiritual friend, like a good therapist, "comforts the disturbed and disturbs the comfortable," but does not stop there. Having traveled the path before you, they point out the pitfalls and breathtaking vistas along the way. But if you project perfection on most teachers, you'll only be disappointed. Many, though they may offer "perfect teachings" for you at the moment, may not be perfected human beings. Applying their words may open great growth, but denying some deeper sense within you that they too have a way to go will turn you away from the "still small voice within." Trust your sense of that teacher. You're probably right. We all are playing at our edge. This is not a competition.

When you begin to treat yourself like your only child, when you have mercy on the crazy mind, when you use life as an opportunity for growth, when you think more in terms of "lightened" than enlightened, when you are committed to stopping nowhere, your path will be clear to go beyond even what I have just said.

When Buddha was dying he said, "Be a lamp unto yourself."

You are the path.

AN EXPLORATION
OF THE MIND

W e watch the mind to see who we *aren't*. Thoughts go by, feelings go by, sensations go by, memories go by; the mind arises and dissolves moment to moment, leaning this way and that. Images arise. Forgotten fragrances. Emotional residues.

Incessant change is our experience—a moment of smelling, changing into a moment of tasting, dissolving into a moment of memory, dissolving to judgement, to wonder, thought, desire, feeling.

Exploring the mind, first its contents, the objects of awareness, are observed—*what* we are smelling, *what* we are thinking about, *what* we are hearing, *what* we remember. We are investigating what we call "ourself"—our thoughts, feelings, desires, fears. We explore "our mind."

Then as we become familiar with this ever-changing mental imagery, able to approach even the most resistant of our unhealed holdings, some modicum of balance begins to discover the quality of change itself. Observing how thoughts end, how even the most "personal" of images and feelings arise quite mechanically and completely uninvited, we begin to explore "the mind." We experience directly the constant unfolding of content as it creates process. And we enter the flow of consciousness itself. Process becomes the focus.

When process is explored we see that anger is not a single state of mind but a multiple unfolding: a moment of frustration, a moment of wanting, a moment of pride, a moment of fear, a moment of worry, a moment of doubt, a moment of distrust, a moment of aggression. And that all states of mind are such.

And we see how object after object is illuminated by the light of awareness, creating consciousness.

And eventually we investigate the space it's all happening in and awareness itself becomes the object of awareness. We explore the Great Mind.

Exploring the mind, all we see is the passing show of conditioning. All we see is old mind. The observed is the observer. And we recognize life in a brand-new way. Needing neither to escape nor grasp for more. Simply a seeing, a directly entering into our lives, a joy beyond our imagining.

There is an unexpected dynamic to all of this. The more we let go, the deeper the experience of the underlying reality, the enormous am-ness in which our tiny thoughts float.

This empty matrix thinks itself
solid and outloud—
and loves itself too small—
floating in the light.

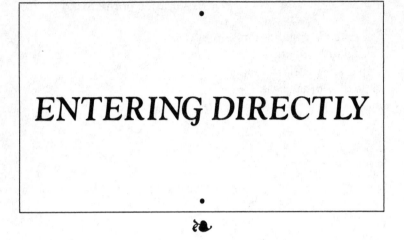

ENTERING DIRECTLY

To enter our lives directly is to braille our way into the center of this very moment. To paraphrase the fifth Zen patriarch, the experience of what we call "our life" is like lightning in a summer cloud. Usually the flash is recognized from a distance, and we are grateful for any light at all. Healing toward the light we recognize how unsatisfactory it is to live life "from afar," to have our living suchness distanced by old mind ways of perception. We seldom see how we are seeing.

But eventually the pain of living life as a "middleman" between the frightened, posturing mind and the patient, spacious heart is more dualism than even the natural schizophrenic tendency of the alternately loving and hating mind, can stand. We ache to be whole.

Then the deep awareness of the heart approaches through the mist and rolling fog of our conditioning which diffuses the light. Ultimately we enter the lightning itself, and beyond, to the very energy from which light is emitted.

Usually we reflect off the moment, rather than on it. The mind bounces from object to object. Awareness seldom enters. Rarely do we know we are thinking when we are thinking. Instead, we are *lost* in thought, mistaking the bubbles for the bath water.

Old mind is like a frightened general posturing well behind the lines, seeking safety in his dress uniform, pretending history. Interpreting rather than entering the moment. Censuring news of the killing fields as well as the bright vistas of heaven.

To enter directly the moment one must penetrate whatever limits direct perception. To enter directly, one needs explore that which seeks to limit exploration. The first stage of entering directly often deals with the resistance to that directness. Fear contorts the moment, and doubts all but its suffering.

To enter directly one needs enter first what limits that entrance. First we directly enter resistance, our deep desire to stay numb and asleep.

Having opened to our closedness, everything becomes fair game. Only then can we begin to explore the body, to receive sensation directly. Meeting sensation moment to moment in the heart of awareness. Seeing that even "the body" is just another thought in the mind. And that the direct experience of body is not one of concept or thought, of "arms" or "legs" or "head," but of a flickering field of sensations.

Entering directly "*my* body" we gradually go beyond the separate to "*the* body," shedding helplessness and isolation. We enter the body we all share.

When we enter directly the sensations that comprise the "flickering body," we get a sense of the vast space in which these sensations are born, tremble, and die. We watch the whole body, the whole mind, thought and sensation, taking birth and dying instant to instant in the Real Body, the body of awareness.

Experiencing directly the nature of the flickering body we are encouraged to approach yet more deeply and explore the uncharted realms of the mind. Magellan on a meditation cushion. No longer settling for others' travelogues, exploring directly.

At first, intimidated by the wild woods of the mind, we slowly begin to investigate the great green canopy. Then focusing, we explore each leaf and blade of grass. Examining the dark furrows in the bark and the fine grain beneath. Entering directly the underbrush of the mind. Recognizing that it isn't just the wild woods of consciousness that is the problem, but the tended gardens, the clearings hacked away, the deeply rooted stumps still an obstacle in the dark. It is not the shriek of our pain that hinders so much as the subtle whispers of the fear that maintains the suffering. Sitting very still in these deep woods we observe how desire betrays clear perception. We see that we are frightened of the possibility of freedom. Our underlying enormity terrifies us. We fear that freedom is beyond our control. We dread being unchained from familiar bonds and excuses. We keep from frightening ourselves by staying so small and afraid.

When we recognize resistance in its subtle movements and complaints, we cut through the densities of old mind and enter directly the fear that is the foundation of our resistance. We enter moment to moment the subtlties of our dread and longing for safety. We watch cell by cell the holding that turns pain to suffering. And we let go into the center of the universe.

And ultimately we watch the "watcher." We enter perception directly, unconditionally, choicelessly investigating how little we have explored.

For the ancient Hebrews, God was only barely approachable. One could be in the presence but could not merge and "be one with God." To find God, shared being, one need only reflect on nature and the nature of nature. But to *be* God one must enter directly that essence in which floats even the seeker of God. Then we don't "know" the truth, we are it.

The idea the "Real Body" is as unreal as any thought floating through. Or perhaps I should say it is as real as any thoughts, but no realer! But the Real Body itself is not a concept. It cannot be known by the unknowing mind; the imagination, the underdream. To think about the Real Body is just thinking; confused and separate, attempting ownership. A shadow in a dream. But to enter directly our own great nature, our "real" nature, is to be liberated from the bonds of our mistaken identity. And to know that who we really are cannot be expressed in words. Our real nature simply isn't small enough to fit within the confines of the mind. And the space, the enormous space of being—how can this tiny mind describe, like a bubble on a moving wave, the ocean on which it floats? But when the bubble bursts (with love and wisdom) it becomes the ocean.

INVESTIGATING MINDFULLY THE MOMENT

Mindfulness is the quality of awareness with which we relate to the contents of the mind, just as heartfulness is the quality of mercy and loving kindness with which we respond to the needs of the world. When mindfulness is well-developed, the heart and mind are one.

To enter the moment directly so that life is not experienced simply as an afterthought, as a partial memory of the previous instant, is to deepen presence. Presence is the quality of not being tardy for our lives.

A Gradual Awakening was written to elucidate the subject of mindfulness practice. It offers more fully the means by which this very instant can be wholly appreciated. It explores ways in which thinking can be seen as thought, how pain can be seen as individual sensations; and feelings can be recognized as multiple changing states of mind. Mindfulness is a means of breaking the seeming solidity of the underdream to awaken directly into the moment which is life.

In recognizing that much of what distorts life into dream is our closed identification with thinking and feeling (and the afterthought of self which makes it all seem so real), we focus on the breath to bring the attention into the present at the level of flowing sensation. Sensations are not thoughts; they are the wordless physically felt characteristics of being in a body constantly changing. They are the perfect backdrop against which to view even the slightest motion in the mind.

To tune to the level of sensation at which breath is always to be found is not to be lost in thinking or emotional reaction. Able to respond directly, to see thought as a bubble floating through, to see feelings like clouds in a vast summer sky, we build an appreciation for the moment. Here nothing is distraction and all becomes perfect grist for the mill of awakening.

One can watch the breath at either the nostrils or the belly. The Soft-Belly Mindful Breathing meditation explores the belly breath. I watched at the belly for five years before changing quite consciously to the nostrils. Each has its advantages. Neither is superior. In each all has to be done. The important thing about choosing the belly or the nostrils is not to vacillate back and forth during meditation. One chooses either and stays there for five years, watching even suggestions from the restless mind to look elsewhere. There is nowhere else to go. All the work that is to be done is done by the awareness itself, not the object of awareness.

Let the attention become present at the belly or nostrils so as to feel the passage of each breath uniquely. Watch the multiple sensations that make up each in-breath. Notice the space between each and how nature abhors a vacuum: thoughts rush in, images arise. Notice the complete out-breath. Its beginning, its middle, its end. Whole breath in whole awareness. Few at first can stay with even a half-dozen consecutive breaths because as thoughts whisper through, and images are overlaid on the screen of consciousness, the mind tends to wander off and follow them into dream. But there are no distractions when one is awakening to life. Each moment is seen uniquely as is, perfectly presenting itself in clear and choiceless awareness. The awareness neither moves toward nor pulls back from anything. No clinging or condemning. Even judgement is noticed as just another nervous tic in the long-conditioned persona, its ancient "flight or fight" syndrome, its ever-fatiguing liking and disliking of what arises on the screen.

To be mindful means to acknowledge what is happening while it is happening. Mindfulness does not attempt to control the ever-changing weather of the mind, but instead cleans the windows of our seeing to gauge whether it is a good day for a ride in the country or if our time is best spent at home (in the heart) tidying up loose ends.

Becoming mindful of the breath, we enter into our existence at the level of sensation, noticing instantly all that is other than sensation—the least thought is recognized at its inception, the heaviest state met in its fragile infancy. Everything is recognizable in a blameless watching of what is as it is. Noticing the deep tendencies for control and judgement within a developing stillness, one watches without comment the passing show. As awareness explores the most noticeable activities of the mind/body, it gradually becomes refined, able to hear the sublest whispers of thought, feeling, and sensation, to discover the breath inside the breath, the thought within thinking, the feeling within feelings. Awareness breaks the illusion of someone thinking, watching our "someoneness," and recognizes it as just another bubble on the breeze.

It returns gently the wandering attention again and again to the breath, acknowledging and noting all that arises.

Not surprised by the subtle fears and doubts that flicker through. Developing courage and patience, concentration and mindfulness, openness and clarity. Just as the attention might need to be brought back to soften the belly dozens of times an hour, so awareness is returned again and again from passing thoughts that momentarily interpose themselves between awareness and the breath (arising feelings, associated memories, fantasized futures) to the coming and going sensations of the breath.

To help us stay present, we employ a gentle acknowledgment, a *noting* of what is as it is. When thinking arises, note silently from the heart "thinking"; when fear, "fear." Recognizing that each moment fully accepted for itself has little to attract identification or suffering. Acknowledging a moment of judgement has little to instigate further judging. Noting judgement allows it to remain unjudged, even "appreciated" for its capacity to fractionalize the mind.

To stay present to the shifting contents of the moment, many use this technique to acknowledge the contents of the mind as a silent whisper in the heart, noting "judging" when judgement passes through the mind, or "doubt" when distrust resists, or "anger" when the jaw has tightened like rawhide and the teeth clamped down, or the ever-changing quality of the state of fear as it occasionally meanders through. When we see these qualities for what they are then "fear" does not frighten, "judgement" does not judge, "joy" does not leave us joylessly grasping for more. Each thing is as it is, and all become workable.

But here again one must watch old mind's tendencies. The purpose of the technique is not to lock into the breath but to use the breath as a means of tuning to the present. Practice establishes a direct relationship to the breath. If the mind should find the momentum of fear or doubt continuing of itself, by itself, one does not struggle with the breath but allows awareness to enter wholly into the moment-to-moment unfolding of that state. Just as one has attempted to gently stay with the moment-to-moment changes within the in-breath and out-breath, cultivating a choiceless awareness. Mindfulness of joy is not a quicker way to heaven than mindfulness of anger. No object of mindfulness is preferable to any other, or offers any more freedom. Heaven is too small for our Real Body, for our true nature; indeed, the kingdom of heaven is within that. Holding to any moment passed we exchange the living truth for the overscripted underdream.

We can find great awakening watching such states of mind as boredom or anger. Indeed, for many it is a relatively advanced stage in their mindfulness before the pleasant will be watched with the same acuity as the unpleasant. To be able to stay with the moment-to-moment unfolding of rapture with that same even-minded open-heartedness may take a while because its seductive nature draws us into identification. We become lost in pleasure.

Everything that arises in mindfulness becomes a perfect mirror for us to go beyond our ancient addiction to the contents of the mind and be able to receive the awareness reflected back from each object; to become conscious of awareness itself so identification does not entrap any object in the mind, neither ecstasy nor grief. No longer mistaking the objects of awareness for awareness itself, like the sun recognizing its own light reflected from the moon, our true nature is revealed.

For some, old mind may complain that an ongoing mindfulness of the passing show might suppress spontaneity. But much of what we call spontaneity is actually a compulsive twitch. When we are wholly present, unseen alternatives arise that increase the breadth of action rather than narrow it. It is not hypnosis but rather "de-hypnosis," as a friend long ago pointed out. Although it may sound as though one would "flatten" experience, in truth one opens to yet subtler and subtler levels of being, discovering that what we always experienced as the "aliveness" of thought is actually the scintillation of the awareness which receives it.

The unconscious becomes conscious because nothing censors even the least arising of suppressed material. And nothing limits the unlimited. No words can describe the absolute joy, freedom, and peace of a liberated mind. It is synonymous with the open heart. Nothing obstructed, no one suffering.

Many on the path have told us that saying, "Watch breath, soften belly, open heart," has become a wake-up call for mindfulness and mercy, which has taken them beyond the mind/body of suffering into the deep peace of their healing.

This focusing on the breath may be difficult at the beginning. We have cultivated so little concentration and so little mindfulness in the past. At first it may be difficult to stay with even a single in-breath without getting lost in the daydream of planning mind, judging mind, desiring mind. But gradually, patiently, this focus is developed equally. And with it a willingness to receive the moment as it is. What's the rush?! Once one has one's feet on the path of healing, life takes on new meaning and time is no longer the enemy. Each step becomes every step, the healing within liberation, the possibility of freedom. And life becomes exciting. This moment-to-moment awareness, encouraged and focused, allows one to meet the pleasure and pain in the mind/body and participate directly in what exists without adding fears or projections. It is looking oneself directly in the eyes, meeting oneself as if for the first time each time. It means entering the flow of constant change: the pulsations, the tingling, the heat, the cold, the hardness, the softness experienced as body. It is an investigation of the sensations themselves as they are generated at the point of inquiry. It is a probing of the very basis of the experience we call life, an examination of even perception itself and the filters through which all that is sensed is drawn. It means approaching life anew, without models or preconceptions. Entering the moment with a choiceless, merciful awareness, an openhanded receptivity which seeks nothing except to experience life as is.

It means approaching the moment at the ground zero of "don't know." Letting go of preconceived attitudes, the colored lenses through which we have seen or hardly seen for so long. Seeing and examining seeing. Feeling and examining feeling. Watching and examining the watcher. It is entering directly into one's life. It means unconditionally watching the conditioned. It means, in searching for the sacred vastness, that we watch the mind to see who we aren't.

In seeing things as they are, the grasping identifications of old mind diminish. More and more, objects of consciousness are allowed to float in clear awareness. Less and less, objects of consciousness are mistaken for all we are. Gradually, awareness itself may be directly experienced, seeing the very process out of which consciousness arises. Going to the very root of consciousness we meet anew our primordial nature.

When we see how difficult it is to "just watch the breath," we see the nature of what many call "monkey mind." The mind like a monkey swinging through the trees, propelled by its grasping from limb to limb—moved through the forest of the mind by its continual reaching out for the next object to swing from—the exquisite beauty of the forest canopy a blur of motion, indistinct, unknown.

When awareness is repeatedly encouraged to gently return to the moment, it looks straight ahead and all is seen as arising and passing away. The continual impermanence of all we have been grasping at for so long at last recognized in its most minute detail. Without the least need to change our way of being, awareness changes it all by itself and a new path comes up to meet each step.

As concentration develops, awareness receives previously unnoticed realms of being. Then the journey seems not somewhere we are going but an increasing appreciation of where we are. All that we have sought is found in this very instant.

Old mind is monkey mind. Old mind is thinking. Old mind is compulsive reaction to unexplored stimuli. It is the uninvited, the mechanical, the moment as dream, as a blur of confusion and suffering. New mind is "just this much." It is a new heartfulness in which the mind need not be different but is related to in a wholly different way. It is the mind sunk wholly into the heart. It is life renewed, life as healing.

It is said, "If you can see 'just this much,' you can see everything." If we can fully open to this millisecond, this moment of existence, all will be revealed. If life is lived as just this moment, life will be lived to its fullest. But if "just this much" is not enough, life will be insufficient and old dreams will beckon.

There are as many ways of practicing mindfulness as there are of playing the piano. As one learns, for instance, to play the piano, one may be constantly "waiting for the time when I can really play" or, a bit more present, one may enjoy the practice for itself: the daily increase in facility and the ability to express oneself. The joy of music. One may bang impatiently on the keys, waiting for the music to begin, or one may be enthralled, experimenting with the same note over and over again to "grok" the nature of "piano." Some enjoy each moment of practice, others can't wait to be virtuosos. And, of course these are not two other people but two aspects of us each.

So too there are numerous ways in which mindfulness may be applied. Some impatiently attack the mind, insisting that it be different than it is. Others, with a deep sigh of recognition, softly smile at the joy of each moment of letting go, of direct seeing. The tendency to attack the objects of the mind and attempt to overcome them, to force clarity, can cause us to focus on the mind in a way that one long-time meditator called "mercilessly attentive." This war with the mind can make one impatient and goal-oriented and create more self, more suffering. But in receiving, rather than attacking, the objects perceived, we gradually move beyond the mind, beyond death, beyond even "being" to the indescribable spaciousness of beingness itself.

The attempt to try to escape our suffering instead of entering our pain is seen in the tendency of some meditators to "strike" the objects of the mind with an intention of making them vanish. This "hardening" of practice can make one feel uneasy with life, and quite uneasy with oneself. In softening to practice, the objects of the mind are more appreciated for their emptiness than attacked for their solidity. Perception floats, well received. In this attitude of gentling toward the mind, we approach the process appreciatively, and cultivate the mercy necessary to open the pathway to the heart. When practice is as light as the breath within the breath, there is a profound element of mercy that shines within a choiceless receptivity. It does not force change but simply allows it. Indeed, it watches the tendency to force things patiently, without alarm or condemnation.

As one teacher said, "Don't be a Buddhist, be a Buddha. Don't be a Christian, be Christ. Don't be a meditator, meditate!" "I" is a verb, not a noun. There is more to our liberation than just meditation. As this teacher pointed out, "Don't leave your practice on the meditation cushion!" It is an offering to the suffering of the world. It is inner preparation for the Great Healing, the liberation of all sentient beings "unto the last blade of grass."

When mindfulness has been cultivated, a merciful awareness meets the world as a wide-eyed pilgrim. It does not judge or become surprised by anything. Nothing takes it unawares. It simply watches, not from some "center," some "point of view" that easily gives rise to an idea of there being a "watcher," just more self to suffer—but from within a spacious awareness that appreciates the passing process, opening from moment to moment into the "sure heart's release."

For more about how this practice works in the healing process, see Healing into Life and Death.

A SIMPLE MINDFULNESS MEDITATION— FOCUSING ON THE BREATH AND NOTING

(To be read slowly to a friend or silently to oneself.)

Find a comfortable place to sit with the back straight but not rigid.

Allow the body to breathe naturally. Bring the attention to the nostrils where the touch of the breath is most noticeable.

Bring awareness to the sensations produced by the air, passing in and out of the nostrils.

Keep the attention at one precise point. Note the sensation that accompanies each breath. When breathing in note "in." When breathing out, note "out." Let noting keep you on the track, in the present. It is not a thinking about what is but a simple acknowledgment, whispered by the heart to the mind.

Let awareness settle into the level of sensation.

If the attention wobbles, bring it back to the sensations present at the nostrils.

To aid recognition of what is happening while it is happening note silently the state which drew awareness away, "thinking." If judgement arises, note simply "judging."

Note "in," when breathing in; note "out," when breathing out, to help stay with the tides of the breath. Note the process of breathing that these sensations comprise. Note the breath passing in and out of the nostrils.

Do not think the breath. Don't even visualize it. Just be present for the sensations that spontaneously arise with each unique breath. Mindfulness of breathing.

Sounds that arise are noted as "hearing, hearing." Thoughts are noted as "thinking"; other sensations that arise are noted as "feeling" or "sensation." Let the language be natural and your own. Most is noted—arising and passing away—in the process; vanishing before it can even be labeled.

In the moment-to-moment awareness of the silent sensations coming and going with the breath there is no grasping or pushing away. There is a simple, merciful openness to what is.

Just a clear, precise, gentle observation of the breath.

Sensations arise in the body. Thoughts arise in the mind. They come and go like bubbles.

Each mind-moment is allowed to arise and allowed to pass away of its own momentum. No pushing away of the mind; no grasping at the breath. Just gently returning awareness to the sensations always present with the coming and going of the breath. Gently returning.

The awareness of breath is foreground. In the background, everything else floats by as it will.

Each breath unique—sometimes deep, sometimes shallow, always slightly changing. The whole breath is felt going in, stopping, and coming out. The whole breath is experienced at the level of sensation, of touch. Noted

*entering and leaving the nostrils. "Breathing in"; "breath-
ing out."*

*Breathing just happens by itself. Awareness simply
watches. Belly soft. Face relaxed. Shoulders loose. No
holding anywhere. Just awareness and breathing.*

*Just consciousness and the object of consciousness,
arising and passing away moment to moment in the vast
space of mind.*

*Don't get lost. If awareness wanders, return gently,
without judging, or clinging, to the breath. Notice the
whole breath, from its beginning to its end, precisely,
clearly, from sensation to sensation.*

*The body breathes by itself. The mind thinks by itself.
Awareness simply observes the process without getting lost
in the content. Note "thinking" and return to the "in" and
"out" of the breath.*

Each breath unique. Each moment completely new.

*If sensation should arise in the body, let the awareness
recognize it as sensation. Notice it coming and notice it
going. Not thinking it as "body" or "leg," or "pain." Simply
note this moving energy as "sensation" and return to the
breath.*

*The whole process occurring by itself. Awareness ob-
serving, moment to moment, the arising and passing away
of experiences in the mind and body. Moment-to-moment
change. Moment to moment acknowledgement of change.*

*Awareness of sensation coming and going by itself. Just
breath, and awareness of breath.*

*Surrender to the breath. Experience the breath. Don't
try to get anything from it. Just allow awareness to penetrate to the level of sensations that arise of themselves and
by themselves.*

*The point of touch becomes more and more distinct,
more intense with the coming and going of each breath.*

*The mind becoming focused on the sensations that
accompany breathing.*

If thoughts arise, clearly note their motion in mind, rising and passing away like bubbles. Notice them, and return to the mindfulness of the breathing. "Thinking, thinking."

If feelings predominate, note softly what presents itself as "anger," or "fear," or "doubt" or "wanting." And return gently to the breath.

Observe thought as it enters and passes away; feeling or sensation as it comes into being and dissolves.

Don't think about how to note thinking. Just let noting note for itself.

If noting should start to get in the way, to create more thinking, just let it go and return wholeheartedly to the breath. Just a clear awareness of what predominates in the mind or body as perception arises.

Return deeply to the area of sensation that marks the passage of each breath.

Subtler and subtler sensations momentarily predominate. Thoughts predominate. Each noted clearly within a concentrated awareness.

Watch mind's motion, its continual change from object to object, breath to breath, sensation to sensation.

Moment-to-moment objects arise and pass away in the vast space of mind, and body. An easy, open awareness simply observes the process of arising and passing away. Returning to the sensations of the breath.

Feelings arise a bit more clearly. Thoughts arise with more precision—the "planning mind," the "judging mind." Awareness experiences the process of their movement. Not lost in content. Observe thought passing through the vast space of mind.

These words arising from nothing; disappearing into nothing. Just open space in which the whole mind, the whole body, are experienced as moment-to-moment change.

Sound arises and passes away.

Feeling arises and passes away.

All of who we think we are, moment to moment, coming and going, bubbles in space, arising and passing away in the vast openness of a merciful awareness.

A NOTE ON NOTING

Noting is a silent acknowledgment in the heart of what is occurring in the mind. Noting simply states what is without the least intention to interfere. It encourages an openness to healing. It cultivates qualities of honesty, non-judgement, awareness of the contents of consciousness, and an ongoing sense of presence in the present. It brings the practice from the meditation pillow into the world. It aids in generating a continuity of awareness. It keeps the mind in touch with the body. It is a direct recognition of the moment.

When thinking draws awareness to itself, one notes silently "thinking, thinking." In the beginning of this practice the grossest evident state of mind and body will be easily labeled as "thinking" or "feeling" or "pain" or "resistance." Later, as the process of noting becomes refined and takes on a quality of subtler recognition, one might find it

natural—without thinking a label, to just note spontaneously the qualities therein—instead of noting "thinking,"
one might notice "planning" or "doubting" or "loving" or
"fearing."

The degree of a thought's "power of attraction" to
awareness is called "attachment." Tens of thousands of
mind-moments flash through awareness from instant to
instant but only a few have the density and magnetic
attraction to arise fully into consciousness as a thought.
That magnetic propensity that originates from one's personal, and inherited, history is the degree to which we have
"work" with the object of that thought. There is both
positive and negative attachments. A grasping or resistance
that reacts to any object of awareness passing through.
Noting attachment—noting "liking" and "disliking" from
object to object—keeps us aware of "the chain of events."
Indeed there is a method of mindfulness that deals not only
with watching sensations, thoughts and feelings against the
silent backdrop of physical sensation, but is primarily
focused on noting the liking and disliking that arises in the
mind from moment to moment.

Noting keeps awareness on the track. It is a recognition
of the weather of the mind. It senses when there is an 80
percent chance of rain today or when the clouds are
parting. It feels the first rays of the sun. As well as the first
drop of rain. It is present in the present. It receives a
snowflake in an open palm, not in a fist jammed deep
within a lint-lined pocket.

Noting is a process of identifying a state of mind before
we identify *with* that state. Recognizing a swamp before we
are sunk up to our hips in the ooze. Though it may take a
while to integrate noting into our daily experience, it
eventually becomes a lighthearted recognition of occasional
heavyheartedness. We begin to meet the world with a new
healing. Nothing takes us by surprise. We have explored
our hindrances and we meet them with the light-hearted

ease of "Big surprise, fear again, anger again, resistance again."

Noting becomes a gentle acknowledgment of the passing show. It recognizes and notes change as it occurs. It allows content to be seen within the larger context of process. And eventually process in the enormous context of being, the sacred emptiness of our essential nature, the boundaryless heart.

Noting means nothing added. It means "just this much," the moment as it is. The millisecond in which truth is to be found. Noting is not even a subvocalization. It arises at the moment of perception, before interpretation changes experience to a personal memory. As one longtime meditator said, "It is the meditator's world companion. When you know where you are, you are always at home."

Noting takes the meditation "off the cushion" and into our everyday lives. It is with us throughout our daily changes. It recognizes when we are moving toward or pulling away from the moment. It is with us when we drive, when we eat, when we work. It is like an old friend reminding us to pay attention.

Eventually noting becomes a spontaneous response to changing states. Noting with a simple easiness the flow of consciousness. Not thinking about or analyzing this state in order to label it—not creating more thinking.

Acknowledging the flow of consciousness: "planning," "doubting," "hoping," "wondering," "fearing," "enjoying," "liking," "disliking," "envying," "loving," "hating," "longing," "pride," "jealousy," "enthrallment," "joy."

If noting gets in the way, discard it. It is only a technique. When the mind is of itself on track and clear, noting may be "something extra" and leave a trace that it is not useful. If noting at times feels to be more a hindrance than an ally, encouraging the analytical tendency rather than a simple presence—more work than clear play—drop it.

As the practice of noting enters deeply and becomes one's own, the words tend to fall away and just a recognition of changing content maintains itself. The effort to become effortless has once again paid off. Then perhaps noting will only be employed for the heavy, more afflicting, states we recognize we sometimes become lost in. Noting perhaps "fear" or "doubt" or "distrust" or "joy" so as not to be swept away by these more intense unfoldings. But generally just a mindfulness notes what is, wordlessly, no longer a "labeler" or even a "watcher" but instead, having entered directly the process, the watching itself.

LETTING GO INTO CONSCIOUS LIVING

Conscious living, like conscious dying, allows us to let go of the last moment and open to the next. As contact with the breath is developed over some weeks of relating to the breath wholeheartedly and returning the attention to the sensations at the nostrils each time that thinking or feeling or other bodily sensations draw it away, we come to know the nature of the swing of awareness from object to object and increasingly we find ourselves in the immediate present.

As attention becomes able to let go lightly of whatever shiny object has attracted it: letting go of judgement without judging, letting go of fear without being frightened, letting go of pride without being proud, one learns the liberating power of letting go.

In each moment of letting go, patience and mercy deepen. Relinquishing momentary holding opens the heart. In the moment of letting go of thought or feeling, of doubt or rapture, to return to the sensations of the breath, we cultivate a willingness to go beyond old mind's holding, trusting the "don't know" wonderment of the next moment arising.

In each moment of letting go, we enter our birth and ease our death.

Watching closely each moment of letting go, we let things be as they are without the least force or need to be otherwise and, returning from thinking, notice thought as a bubble floating through the vast spaciousness of awareness. A fragile bubble on whose thin film is reflected our dream world and the environs of the mind.

Each moment of letting go intensifies the possibility of further freedoms. And conditions our response to the next arising of feeling and thought. Each moment of letting go of fear lightens the next moment's experience of fright. Each moment of allowing sensations to float unhindered in the body of awareness, letting them come and letting them go, conditions our ability to respond rather than react to the next sensation, whether it is pleasant or not, liked or disliked.

In each moment of letting go, lightning passes through the mind/body.

When the moment of letting go has been explored with the same sensitivity as the breath, as thinking, as feeling, as expectation, as disappointment, one can then develop this quality of letting go into a deeper sense of letting be, of being itself.

At this point, when thoughts turn into thinking and expectation turns into planning, awareness acknowledges clearly these states as they are investigated.

If a thought or feeling repeatedly interjects itself after having been let go of again and again to return to the breath, and continues unabated, awareness is then encouraged to wholly let go of the breath and enter directly into the state, to explore its motion and density thoroughly, its ever-changing quality, its process. Having stabilized the attention in the moment, in the sensations of the breath, one is then able to explore the shadow play of the moment. If the attention is repeatedly lured away from the breath by a memory, a feeling, a desire, a line of thought, some chain of events, awareness is placed wholly within that unfolding process to discover its most intimate nature and allow the familiarity which encourages letting go.

If, having let go of the breath to examine a process that momentarily predominates in the mind or body, the mind begins to wander away from its new focus as well, sailing off through the mental catalogue of old laundry lists and days gone by, the activity of this wandering is clearly noted. And, with a precious letting go, we return once again to the sensations at the nostrils to clear the fog.

Noticing that it may be as difficult to stay with the interposing thought or feeling as it was with the illusive breath, awareness is encouraged to receive what is, as it is, with as much mindfulness as it can muster. A mindfulness of breathing becoming the foundation for our presence in the unfolding moment so that all that enters through the mind and body is received in clarity and mercy.

Then we are not fighting with the mind, distracted, or struggling toward the breath. Instead, we are open to all that arises in its very inception. Thoughts being born and dying moment to moment. Birth and death received by that which goes beyond even life. Consciousness expanding from moment to moment into the space opened by our letting go. When we have let go of everything only the truth remains.

Coming back again and again to the living present, we watch the content of the mind floating in the deathless, the uninjured, the ever whole. Not mistaking the objects of awareness for awareness itself. Exploring equal-mindedly, openheartedly, openhandedly all that arises as it arises.

Watching the breath minutely at the nostrils, its slightest comings and goings, the whispered intentions beneath, the least movement anywhere in the mind/body is instantly recognizable. Developing a choiceless, "let go," awareness, no object of exploration is preferable to any other. Each is allowed fully to arise and dissolve in a non-interfering mercy and awareness.

Deepening mindfulness of the process unfolds without grasping at understanding or attempting to force healing. Insight and well-being arise naturally. In the merciful softness, "a willingness to be" receives the breath. And choicelessly allows the mind to manifest as it will, healing at levels not previously accessible.

And in the subtle whispers of the mind, intention is recognized preceding each movement of the body, each action in the world. Seeing the desire to scratch that leads to scratching allows insight into the cues from the mind that motivate each action. Intention, the middleman between desire and compulsive activity, noticed at its inception, heard clearing its throat. The tendency toward unconscious reaction, the chain of events, broken in the clear light of an awareness that seeks nothing but the moment.

Awaking from the mechanical quality of our life, from the constant implosion and explosion of the mind in the body, in the world, we may even get a glimpse of our true nature, a millisecond of healing that lasts a lifetime.

In watching the ever-becoming of the mind floating in this space of constant being, we break our addiction to the mistaken identity of our suffering and receive life in the very instant of its unfolding. In the deathless nature of the underlying reality.

A GUIDED MINDFULNESS MEDITATION

(To be read slowly to a friend or silently to oneself.)

Let the attention come into the body.
Let it settle to the level of sensations generated there.
Feel the buttocks as they press against the chair.
Feel the hands folded in the lap.
Allow awareness to experience the multiple sensations arising and disappearing in rapid succession in the body.
A moment of pressure here, an instant of sensation there.
Just receive the body as it is.
Just feel this body breathing all by itself.
And gradually allow the attention to come to these sensations generated by breath in the body.
Feel these sensations in the belly, in the chest, in the throat.
Observe the sensations generated in the body with each inhalation, with each exhalation.
Allow the attention to come fully to the sensations generated by the breath at the nostrils.

Notice where the sensation that accompanies each breath predominates.

Is it felt most clearly at the upper lip, inside the rim of the nostrils, at the tip of the nose?

On whatever sensation is most distinct, focus the awareness.

Let awareness enter sensation.

Notice clearly the quality of change within.

If awareness wanders away from the sensations at the nostrils, lost for a moment in thinking, in planning, in wondering, just notice directly and without judgement where awareness went and, gently letting go, return to the sensations of the breath at the nostrils.

If judgement arises, notice that too—without judgement. Observe directly the involuntary process of uninvited judging.

Watch the process unfolding all by itself. Let it come. Let it go. And return gently to the breath.

Establish the attention at the nostrils like a watchman stationed at the gates of a city.

Let awareness consider each sensation that accompanies the breath.

No force, no leaning toward the breath, just an allowing awareness which receives multiple changing sensations with each in-breath, with each out-breath.

Mindfulness of breathing.

As the changing flow of sensation is recognized, let the awareness become a bit more focused.

Notice too the space between the inhalation and exhalation. Watch for any thought arising. See how thought thinks itself and return to the breath.

Notice even the subtle intention to inhale or exhale that arises just before the top of the in-breath or the bottom of the out-breath.

If you notice any intention, any desire, to control the breath, just note this tendency and allow the breath to breathe itself in clear awareness, that moment floating in a merciful receptivity.

Allow the breath its natural tides.

Holding nowhere.

Simply observing.

Simply receiving experience as it unfolds.

Staying moment to moment with the multiple unfolding sensations in each exhalation.

Noticing the space between breaths and the intention to inhale once again.

Moment-to-moment mind is recognized as words or images silhouetted against the wordless backdrop of sensation. Thoughts arise and dissolve—like shooting stars.

The slightest movement of mind noticed clearly against the silent flow of sensation.

Never has thought been acknowledged so quickly after its arising. Seeing directly the mechanics of thought, thinking does not continue unaware. Mindfulness of thinking.

Letting go of thought, return gently to the breath.

Notice any judgement, any longing, any idea of what should be happening as just more thought, more bubbles floating through the vastness of awareness.

Not thinking the breath, but entering it directly.

Let the awareness go within the breath, feeling moment to moment its subtle change in texture.

As awareness gradually deepens, notice the yet subtler sensations that comprise each moment of the breath process.

Allow the body to breathe all by itself.

No need to control or shape the breath. A keen gentle awareness enters each particle of sensation received.

Notice the beginning, middle, and end of each inhalation.

Observe the space between. Notice the beginning,

middle, and end of each exhalation and the space that follows.

Enter the texture of the breath, feel its smoothness, feel the quality of heat or coolness within each momentary sensation.

Enter deeply the experience of simply breathing.

Without thinking the breath, enter directly its unfolding moment to moment. A direct awareness that simply notes what is without clinging or condemning, without leaning toward or away from the moment. A steadiness that faithfully receives change.

Just exploring sensation at the nostrils.

Where awareness is present, the old is seen in a brand new way.

Just watching.

Just being.

Watch the impermanance of all experience. And, with a gentle letting go, return fully to the breath.

Mindfulness of breathing at the nostrils.

Breathing in, breathing out.

Becoming present in the present by focusing on sensations.

No distractions.

When we are focused on the moment there are no distractions.

Whatever arises is noticed clearly in its changeableness, in its momentary quality dissolving from thought to thought, feeling to feeling, sensation to sensation.

Each moment of thought or feeling or other bodily sensation is simply noted. Recognizing the nature of the process, return, mercifully, gently, to the breath.

When thinking or feeling, draw the attention away from the level of sensation, notice any tension or longing for things to be otherwise. Mindfulness of feelings.

Return, if need be, a dozen times a minute to the breath.

When thinking arises, meet it lightheartedly, noting silently to yourself, "Thinking," "feeling," "planning," "judging."

Just notice whatever arises as it arises and let go gently into the sensations of the breath.

Let go lightly, returning to the breath, noting the beginning, middle, and end of each in-breath.

Noticing the space between breaths.

Noting the beginning, middle, and end of the out-breath and the space between.

Noting texture, exploring any sense of pressure or heat or coolness.

Noting moments of pleasure or displeasure, of liking and disliking from sensation to sensation.

Consciousness receiving the subtle breath breathing itself in the vast spaciousness of awareness.

Note even "someone" watching all this, and just allow watching to watch itself; consciousness unfolding in clear awareness. Mindfulness of process.

Just awareness and sensation meeting moment to moment.

Go beyond even the concept "breath" to enter the flow of consciousness directly.

Enter directly.

Mercifully.

Gently.

Persistently.

Staying with it.

Becoming present in the present.

TAKING THE
FIRST STEP

One of the means, like noting, of bringing our meditation "off the cushion" is to expand our healing into "active meditations."

In walking meditation one no longer attends to the breath but brings that same one-pointed focus on the moment to the experience of walking. The walking meditation is a very simple practice of paying precise attention to the sensations in the hips, legs, knees, thighs, ankles, feet, and toes that arise with each step. It has the same acuity of attention to subtle sensation as is generated in the mindfulness of breath. It is done, at first, very slowly and deliberately—feeling the foot bend off the ground, the leg swing forward, the toes and heel, placed mindfully on the ground. Noting *lifting*, *placing*, *putting* with each step. We are learning to walk all over again. When one is doing this meditation with very close attention to the multiple sensations that arise with each step, it can take several minutes to cross the living room or a millisecond to walk a mile. Where is there to go? And here we are.

Thich Nhat Hanh has written an exceptionally clear book, *A Guide to Walking Meditation*. We highly recommend it.

MEDITATION BLUES

Sometimes it breaks my heart
to watch my mind—
cold self-interest,
insistent fear and judgement,
whispered insults,
vengeful fantasies,
triumph and despair.

A conditioned unfolding
so impersonal,
we take it personally.

Sometimes aghast
at the casual cruelty
of even minor fears
and celebrations.

110

Sometimes it breaks my heart
to watch my mind.

And sometimes it stays broken
long enough to touch
even this pain
with love.

Sometimes the mercy washes
even Mrs. Macbeth's hands,
turns tragedy to grace,
and makes it all worthwhile.

Sometimes it breaks my mind
to watch my heart.

AN EXPLORATION OF HEAVY, AFFLICTIVE EMOTIONAL STATES

Healing accompanies awareness. Our liberation is as deep as our investigation. By cultivating a deep, merciful awareness, healing enters levels of the mind/body previously unexplored.

When the afflictive emotions of what are called "heavy states" momentarily predominate (Big surprise!) and one feels "overwhelmed" by fear, anger, guilt, doubt, confusion, greed, shame, lust, mercilessness, or any of the top 40 "oldies but baddies" of the mind, such an exploration as here suggested might prove quite useful.

Such intense emotional states have a certain hallucinogenic quality about them, an insistence on being "more real" than anything that has passed through lately. A quality of agitation and disquiet that states unequivocally this discomfort shall continue forever, and just get worse. They threaten to burn us to the ground. But they lie! In truth we have never experienced a single emotion or thought that has ever stayed. All are a part of a constantly changing process. Neither the worst feelings we have ever had, nor the best, could be maintained indefinitely. To tune to the process, to the flow of impermanence, in which these feelings unfold, is to break identification with the seeming solidity of "the suffering" as well as "the sufferer."

It may take a while before you can greet the age-old pains of the mind/body with the light acceptance of "Big surprise, you again!" And invite them in for a healing. But it is meditations such as these that establish familiarity and comfort with "the discomforted" and a sense of the workability of even such heavy feelings.

Indeed, the word "feelings" has a double meaning. One is of emotion. The other of sensation. But this is no casual happenstance of language, it is an insight into the correlation between mental experience and its bodily expression. Every emotion and each state of mind has a corresponding body pattern. Palpable configurations which outline the mind state in the body.

Often thoughts of fear, doubt, etcetera, are too seductive, their content too identified with as "*my* fear" or "*my* doubt," to see the process of "*the* fear," "*the* doubt." We just can't get sufficient space around these feelings, so quickly does the trembling mind implode about their imagery.

But by focusing awareness on the bodily expression of these afflictive states we may discover a way through. We may not be able to stay mindful of the thoughts in anger or fear for even a minute before identification seduces us into becoming angry and frightened. But letting the content of thought unfold as it will and directing awareness to enter the body pattern, rather than the thought imagery, of this feeling—the clenched teeth, the hardened belly, the tightened sphincter—we can stay quite present for emotions we often become lost in.

This meditation allows us to lighten the load of heavy emotion, dissolving the threatening solidity of these states by examining one by one their incremental composition in the mind/body.

The quality of exploration cultivated in this meditation allows us to relate *to* these states instead of *from* them. This exploring layer after layer of the seeming solidity of these heavy states could be likened to examining through a microscope a piece of polished stone. At first we discover the considerable porousness of its seemingly smooth surface. Then, focusing deeper, its crystalline structure comes into view. Penetrating into the seemingly solid, we discover the vast space between molecules, an enormous sky in which these scattered constellations glitter. And entering deeper, yet, the cosmic spaciousness of the atom. So much space in so little solidity just like the mind/body. So much room for awareness to infiltrate and experience its own spacious nature even in the midst of the seemingly solid.

A GUIDED EXPLORATION OF HEAVY, AFFLICTIVE EMOTIONAL STATES

(To be read slowly to a friend or silently to oneself.)

*W*hen *identification with dense mental states such as fear, doubt, anger, or pride contract the mind and narrow access to the heart, find a comfortable place to sit and take a few smooth, deep breaths into the body.*

Although the mind has many voices, let its words just float. Watch the momentum unfolding.

Just let thoughts think themselves as the even flow of breath begins to soften the body.

Let the belly soften to receive the moment.

In soft belly we have room for it all.

In this softness allow awareness to roam free in the body, exploring sensations.

Notice any areas of tension or denseness.

Notice areas of pressure or movement.

Of heat or cold.

The tinglings, the vibratory quality.

Softly allow awareness to receive the body.

115

Does this state of mind have a correlation in the body? Is there a body pattern for this emotion?

Feel the sensations that accompany this state of mind as they arise in the muscles, bone, and flesh. Feel the physical imprint of this mental state.

Explore the sensations in the stomach and belly. Is there tension? Holding? Resistance?

Let awareness move gently into the chest. Is the breath constricted? Is there some desire for control which attempts to shape and hold the breath?

Let the attention be drawn to whatever sensations predominate. Explore the body pattern of this state of mind.

What has mind labeled these feelings?

How has it described this experience to itself?

Does it call it fear?

Does it call it anger?

Does it call it joy?

Acknowledge the state of mind. Note it.

Each state of mind has its own particular qualities. What are the qualities of this moment?

Let awareness explore the moment-to-moment process of this feeling in the body.

Are these sensations changing?

Do they move from one area to another?

Is the body pattern of this state enunciated more in one area than another?

In the back or the neck?

In the gut?

What are the sensations in the tongue? Is it pushing against the teeth? Pressed against the roof of the mouth? What holding is exhibited there?

What is occurring at the top of the head?

Noticing, area by area, the mind's expression in the body.

Examine the constant unfolding of thought silhouetted against this wordless presence at the center of sensation.

What are the voices in the mind/body?

Simply listen. Nothing to answer back.

Just receiving.

Note the intonation of these voices, their intensity.

Allow the awareness to settle a bit more deeply into its listening.

Is it an angry voice?

A frightened voice?

A confused voice?

Listen to the tone.

Is there a noticeable intention in the voice?

What is the intention of this state of mind/body, of this emotion, of this aspect of the personality?

Does it make you feel better or worse?

Does it wish you well? Does it take you closer to your true nature? Does it accept you as is?

What might be the effect of bringing forgiveness or love into this mind/body? Would it resist letting go of its suffering?

Is this a voice we wish to take counsel from? Does it lead us to wholeness or defeat?

Is there love in that voice?

Or is there judgement or pity or doubt?

Just listening.

Just receiving the moment as it is.

Do these feelings have a point of view, a direction they insist you travel?

Where is the love? The mercy and kindness?

Where is the healing in their offering?

Now allow the attention to enter into the deep movement within this state.

Feel its energy, its changeability, its process unfolding in space.

Is it a single emotion or is it made up of many different

feelings? Does it display a single mood or is it constantly changing expressions?

Perhaps many feelings are noticed.

A moment of pride dissolving perhaps into a moment of anger.

A moment of aggression dissolving into a moment of self-pity.

A moment of judgement dissolving into a moment of hopelessness.

Each feeling melts, dissolving constantly from one state into the next.

Begin to focus on the process, not simply the content.

Notice the quality of change within this seemingly solid state.

Focus on the movement within.

Let the awareness focus into a moment-to-moment examination of the discrete elements which constitute the flow of this experience. See the multiple tiny thoughts and sensations which form the framework of this experience.

Notice the impersonal nature of these states we took so personally.

Notice how they plead their case.

Notice how they insist they are real and insist they will go on forever, even though they are constantly changing.

Notice the repetitive quality within.

Notice how each voice, each sensation, each feeling, melts automatically, one into the next.

Watch how naturally each thought ends.

Watch how spontaneously the next thought begins.

Observe the next voice, the next feeling arising.

Watch how each state of mind/body is in process, arising and dissolving into the next.

Notice how the "script" is constantly unfolding.

Let it all float in awareness. Let it unfold moment to moment.

Watch how each state arises uninvited. Constantly coming and constantly going.

Watch the incessant birth and death of thought.

Watch how life is constantly unfolding all by itself.

Observe how thoughts think themselves.

Notice how feelings feel themselves.

Give these constantly changing sensations and thoughts a little more space, a little more room to unfold in a soft body and an open heart.

Let the belly breathe all by itself.

The chest clear.

The throat open.

The tongue soft and gentle in the mouth.

Just receiving the moment as it arises without the least clinging or condemning.

Nothing to change.

No one to be.

Just the merciful space of exploration in which the moment-to-moment process unfolds.

All which seemed so solid before is seen constantly dissolving in space.

Not creating the moment, just receiving it.

Watching it all as process unfolding, observing wholeheartedly what is.

Letting each moment of experience arise as it will in a spacious awareness. Floating, constantly unfolding in vast space.

Watching thought come and go in spacious mind.

Letting sensations arise and dissolve in soft body.

Allowing.

Soft belly noticing even the slightest holding.

Soft breath opening around even the least tension.

Receiving.

Observing.

Letting come.

Letting be.

Letting go.
Space for it all.
This moment an opportunity for liberation and healing.
This unfolding, life itself, so precious, so fully lived.

ONE THING AT A TIME
An Experiment in Consciousness

A remarkable way to integrate meditation and awareness practice into our daily lives is to do one thing at a
time. Relating wholly to the job at hand. Concentrating
on a single task. When driving not listening to the radio.
When listening to music not reading or eating. When
eating not reading or watching television. When watching
television not eating or reading. When walking simply to
feel the ground beneath your feet. To walk in a sacred
manner. When eating to feel that which eats eating and to
enter directly the sensations and motivations that condition and direct the process. To be mindful of eating in the
same way one is mindful of walking or breathing. To take
one breath at a time, one step at a time, one bite at a time.
To fully experience "just this much," the moment as it is.

There is a story of two Zen monks who meet by a river.
Each recognizes that the other is from a neighboring

monastery and inquires into the nature of the other's teacher. One monk says, "My teacher is the greatest of all. He can fly, he can walk on water, he can go without breathing for twenty minutes!" The other monk nods slowly and smiles, saying, "Oh, your master is very great indeed. But my master is yet greater: when he walks he simply walks. When he talks he only talks. When he eats there is only eating." One teacher had "powers," but the other had power. Powers are desired only by that within us which feels powerless. Considering the sizable labyrinth of the ego, for most, "the powers" are traps. A much greater miracle is simply to be present in our lives, able to open to the moment, treasuring mercy and awareness.

Indeed we have a Zen master friend who was sitting at the breakfast table one morning eating and reading a newspaper. One of his students, knowing this teaching of one-thing-at-a-time, rebuked the teacher, "You're eating *and* reading! How can you remain one pointed?!" To which the wily and very practical teacher replied, "When I eat and read I *only* eat and read!"

Play it lightly. If there are children in the house it may be nearly impossible to do only one thing at a time. In that case, do only six things at a time. Softening the belly in the midst of a hard day. Or as one mother put it when she saw this practice would be very difficult for her, "My schedule is a mess. I guess it's just a belly day."

Doing one thing at a time helps us remember. When you are washing the dishes, driving to work, changing the baby, digging a trench, cooking supper, making love, thinking a thought, attend to the process at hand. Experiencing the body, the breath, changing states of mind, instant to instant. Living "just this much" at a time.

If "just this much" is not enough, nothing will be enough. To attend to "just this much" is to live in a sacred manner.

"WHAT WAS YOUR FACE BEFORE YOU WERE BORN?" HE ASKED

When the heart bursts into flame
history completely disappears
and lightning strikes the ocean
in each cell.

There, before origins,
when the double helix
is struck like a tuning fork
there is a hum
on which the universe is strung.

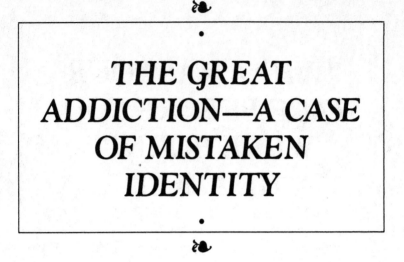

THE GREAT ADDICTION—A CASE OF MISTAKEN IDENTITY

We imagine we are addicted to food or alcohol or sex, but our primary addiction is to the mind. We think we are what we think. We suffer from a case of mistaken identity. We mistake thought for what is thinking. We imagine that every voice, every intention in the mind, is all that is real. We buy into every advertisement that passes through consciousness. We are giant consumers of the mind. We are so easily fooled. We mistake a passing cloud for the immensity of the sky. We keep losing ourselves in thought.

We break our addiction to the mistaken when we investigate the nature of consciousness. As we come to recognize the difference between awareness (am-ness) and an object of awareness (a moment of smelling, tasting, touching, thinking, feeling, hearing), we "come into our own." Experiencing directly how awareness produces consciousness, we don't mistake the former for the latter. We

124

recognize that awareness is the light by which experience is observed, and consciousness is that observation. If awareness is absent, consciousness cannot arise. Consciousness depends on awareness for its existence, but awareness depends on nothing. It is self extant. It is the ground of the universe.

Most don't recognize the difference between consciousness and awareness, just as they don't recognize the difference between thinking and thought.

The more we experience awareness as our true nature, the less we will be seduced by the content of the mind. Awareness breaks the momentum of old conditioning. The more aware we become, the less we are enslaved by our mistaken identity.

Jesus said, "I am the Light." His was the "I am" of our true nature. He never forgot he was God.

BREAKING THE
ADDICTION

We are addicted to the mind. We are dragged along unconsciously by the chain of events. We keep waiting. Our grief overwhelms.

In watching the insistent nature of intention we discover how the "repeated attempt to acquire" is the foundation of the compulsion toward more pleasant sensation, the basis of addiction. A longing for more pleasure and less suffering. Our addiction is to be free of the pain that attends our longing.

"Am-ness" breaks the addiction. "I-ness" takes another drink. In the boundaryless awareness we call "Am-ness" is the healing as well as the cure.

It is said that the only way to break an addiction is to want something else more. When the mind becomes still and the heart turns toward the sacred, even our addictions become grace. Grace is not always pleasant, but it always brings us closer to our true nature.

Addiction casts a battered shadow—assailed by judgement and self-hatred. We are often most merciless with ourselves just when kindness is most needed. Addiction, like any physical pain, is a mirror for our grief. And like any grief we may need first to allow the arms of the Mother of Mercy to enfold us, "All you have to do is put your head on my shoulder." And surrender into the heart of the matter, an alternative to our addiction to the mind, mistaking ourselves for the content instead of the enormity in which it floats.

When we want to be free even more than we want pleasure, when the source of satisfaction, rather than its mirror reflection, is our goal, our addictions become rungs in the ladder we climb to free the pain of our longing and enter the joy of our true nature.

Exploring the urge for lesser satisfactions, we experience the Great Satisfaction. To be free of compulsive desire, we need to desire the end of compulsivity. This is called the "last desire," the Great Desire, the will toward the living truth.

Because our deep desire for completion goes unsatisfied for so long, we settle for success. Or food. Or sex. Or intoxicants. But none satisfies the profoundly unsatisfied for long. We settle for such small desires and just create more of the same. But our deepest desire will not be compromised, it will not settle for lesser gratifications. Only the truth that goes beyond understanding will do. All other desires are consumed by the Great Desire, a yearning for the end of confusion and dulled indifference. The Great Desire eats all other desires. It has no table manners. It plays with its food.

It teaches us to play lightly with lesser leanings. Its priority is a letting go of all that limits letting go. And eventually it dies happily into the heart.

This is no grim relinquishment of pleasure. This is the path of joy. It is the hardest work we will ever do. It is the letting go of our suffering. It allows even desire to float lightly in the vastness of being. It recognizes desire as a given, an uninvited guest with which we shall share our daily lives. Seen as an enemy, the house is torn asunder. Seen as an unexpected pregnancy, we learn to love our offspring. Desire is not the cause of pain, only our identification with desire as "me." When desire is grasped by the "I," all else is lost. But when it is allowed to float, like any natural phenomenon, in the vast am-ness, insight rather than problems arise.

A PERSONAL NOTE
ON ADDICTION

Having said all this about addiction, let me add that nowhere is the statement, "Easier said than done," more applicable. Be gentle with yourself. Perseverance furthers, but a balanced effort to let go of the pain is only gradually acquired. And usually from the heart, long after the mind is defeated in deep despair.

Thirty years ago, driving through city traffic to my heroin connection, pouring sweat and nearly unable to keep down the nausea, enraged at every stoplight, the truth of my pain could no longer be eluded. Enough was enough. I pulled over to the side of the road and just let myself be sick. This could not continue. The heart informed the mind, in no uncertain terms, that it wanted God more. It took years of deadening the space between the heart and mind, with self-administered analgesia, before the heart broke through and stated unequivocally that now was the time to "shit or get off the pot."

It was the Great Desire that saved my ass.

Jung understood perfectly the Great Desire when he directed the founders of Alcoholics Anonymous to add a "Higher Power" to the process. He knew that our healing had to be an ongoing entrance into the heart, a continuous surrender of the pain into the mystery of being. Personally, I find the term *inner power* closer to the truth. Any power imagined outside ourselves can give rise to exactly the codependence we want so to heal.

But before I sound better than I am, let me add, that I too have old habits and holdings, which are only slowly relinquished. They remind me how essential mercy is for working with the addictions so despised by our fragile self-image. Easy does it.

THE CHAIN
OF EVENTS

The chain of events is the process by which desire acts itself out. To watch the mechanics of desire moment to moment is to explore how the energy inherent in desire is transferred from the wanting mind to the active body.

We watch the chain of events link by link, instant to instant, drawing desire into action. Creating unconscious automatic activity.

When we are not aware of the nature of this process, we are dragged through our life by our senses. We live outside ourselves.

Mindful how each link in the chain conveys the energy from unconscious desire to unconscious action, we can learn to unhook desire from automatic activity without suppressing or denying anything. Breaking the chains of unconscious action driven by unexplored desire, we lighten to the tasks at hand. Acting from the appropriate, the heart, rather than from need, the mind.

We are not helpless, only habitual. Awareness melts holding. We have the capacity to watch the chain of events from its very inception. Watching the reception of sensory input—moments of seeing, of hearing, of thinking—we notice, almost before we can name it, a flash of memory informs the mind if that object is pleasant or unpleasant. If pleasant, a leaning toward occurs, which we call "desire." The links are forming. When desire forms in the mind, it inspires an intention to acquire. This motivation informs the body to move toward that object and attempt to grasp it. Intention leads the body toward imagined satisfaction. This volition causes a certain kind of willfulness that employs the problem-solving rational mind to get its way. It is an automatic unfolding but one which can, like eating or breathing, be brought into the light of a clear awareness. Where there is awareness, conditioning is no longer "on automatic."

After observing how perception creates name and form, how memory creates inclination, we watch the chain growing as "liking" stimulates desire. Link by link desire motivates intention. Intention motivating activity. We watch the capacity of desire to move us unwittingly toward what may be unskillful, or even injurious, action. And in this seeing we discover a way to play a bit more lightly with desire. Another opportunity to be a bit more fully alive.

Having explored moment by moment, link by link, this process, we discover the "weak link in the chain." It is intention. When we unhook intention from the automatic process of desire and wanting, the process is interrupted and there is nothing to continue the momentum. Being mindful of intention one notices again and again the "will toward action" that precedes every movement in the body, every action in the world.

All of what is called "karma" is based on intention. It

is this element of consciousness that cultivates and directs all future activity. When there is recognition of intention, our karma is in our hands. We have what seems to be free choice. As a dying friend pointed out, "karma is a wind that is always blowing. It just depends on how you set your sails."

When awareness is focused on the chain of events, habitual reactiveness is de-conditioned, de-magnetized. That which connects the "involuntary" (desire) with the "uninvited" (unconscious activity) is lessened.

Mindfulness breaks compulsive momentum by bringing intention, which links wanting with getting, into full awareness.

Though intention precedes every activity, usually well below the threshold of awareness, as we become a bit quieter the subtle whispers of the mind become more audible. And before we speak, before we take a step, an intention may now and then be noted. What we call "wanting" is already an intention. We want to roll over in bed because we are discomfited. That wanting is the acknowledgment within consciousness of a desire for change. Wanting to get out of the chair we rise automatically, but if we simply noted that intention without acting on it, it would come by repeatedly to catch our attention and motivate us but soon would be seen more as process than anything in need of compulsive reactivity.

Watching the more obvious moments of intention, subtler intentions come into view. We start to get our life back. Mindful of intention, we unhook compulsivity. We de-habituate.

It might be noted here that desire is not "wrong," but only painful. Desire is a sense of not having. A feeling of incompletion until the object of desire is acquired. Desire creates a bending in the mind, a leaning out of this moment, a dissatisfaction with "just this much." The very nature of desire is unsatisfactoriness. It is a longing for a satisfaction that exists in the future. Desire enslaves time. The very nature of wanting is a sense of unfulfillment. Another grief.

So desire is not to be attacked by hatred or moralized by fear but rather explored with mercy and awareness. To understand deeply the nature of desire is to break our bonds.

To play lightly with desire is to enjoy wholeheartedly what is given but not lament what is not.

What does your longing for "French vanilla" create when you come to the ice cream parlor and it is closed? Can you let go lightly? When a lighthearted mindfulness is present we receive our "just desserts." Sweeter than sugar is the freedom of letting go.

Desire is a longing for satisfaction. It is not so much the shiny bauble that we long for so much as the experience we call "satisfaction." The experience of satisfaction is a glimpse of our real nature when it is not obscured by the agitations of desire. Like the sun breaking through clouds we receive for a moment our true nature, the experience of which is pure satisfaction. The satisfaction momentarily experienced when the mind is not leaning out of the moment. When desire is removed by an instant of fulfillment, our underlying nature is revealed. It is the ever-shining, whose character is essential satisfaction. Though desire may lead to momentary satisfaction, its presence in the mind creates a denseness, a thick cloud, which obscures a deeper satisfactoriness—the experience of our underlying suchness.

Our drive to fulfill desire is a kind of backward recognition of the enormity of our light, even a flash of which reminds us why we took birth. All driven by the great longing for that untrammeled spaciousness when desire has momentarily vanished and only the truth remains.

But then other desires to protect that shiny bauble,

that moment of pleasure, rush in to block the reception of further satisfaction and limit the spaciousness of the next moment. "That German shepherd isn't lifting his leg on my new sports car is he!?" Then the object of desire becomes something we desire to protect, something we own, something we fear losing. It is no longer an object of satisfaction but has once again become an object of dissatisfaction.

Exploring the chain of events, we become unchained. Exploring desire and the mechanics of behavior, we get a sense of the liberation that awaits. Moments of clarity increase. We approach "the satisfactory" directly. Without desire acting as "the middleman" we go directly to the source. We enter the enormity of "just this much," no longer navigating by the pained mind but relying on the revealed heart.

ITCHING PLAY
An Experiment in Consciousness

Considerable insight into the workings of desire can be gained by not acting on compulsive volitions. Usually when we itch our hand moves to scratch with very little awareness of what is occurring. To explore the chain of events by which desire is manifest in action, one can investigate the process that occurs when one does not scratch an itch.

When an itch arises (any itch), one first acknowledges the unpleasant. Indeed, by the time one has recognized and acknowledged a moment of unpleasantness, the clever mind has already devised a dozen strategies to relieve and escape the unwanted. In this tiny itch are all the compulsions of a lifetime.

So one sits quietly and takes a moment to oneself. Watching the mind's hand extend again and again to that area of discomfort, attempting relief. Watching the mind's insistence, as repeated intention, we can explore how even the least discomfort, how even minor unpleasantries can become an emergency to the restless mind.

It is a fascinating and wisdom-provoking exercise. It is the beginning of the end of unconscious activity.

This is the sort of play that takes us more playfully toward the essence of being. And the absolute joy of our absolute nature.

AN EXPLORATION
OF EATING

Some say "Food is love," but for many food is self-hatred. With this in mind, be merciful, do not use these meditations as another means of self-abuse and deprivation. But instead as a means of mercifully exploring our relationship to food and eating as a way of freeing the body, mind, and heart to receive nourishment. Enjoy your food mindfully— Taking a Single Bite meditation. And heartfully—Eating in a Sacred Manner meditation.

For many in the "overdeveloped" nations of the world, imbalanced eating is a problem. Food is not taken simply to nourish the body, but as a substitute for deeper nurturings unreceived.

We often eat to feed the hungry ghost in us. Our hunger for pleasure, for praise, for happiness, for sex, for success (here it may be not so much hunger as a kind of indigestion). Because our homesickness for the truth, our

Great Desire, is seldom satisfied, because we don't get what we really want, we settle for fleeting satisfaction.

We are born hungry and frightened, with absolute joy the birthright of our absolute nature.

To turn that frightened ghost, the ever-hungry shadow, into the holy ghost, the sacred breath, is the freedom we seek. Liberation occurs when the ghost becomes pure spirit.

Exploring any hunger leads to the liberation of all hungers. Of hunger itself, *the* hunger which drives *the* pain. In an odd way our hungers are nothing personal, but they lead to a sense of personal dismay.

If we undertake to investigate any process which is automatic, such as breathing or eating, we create an opportunity to bring the involuntary within the realm of the volitional and a merciful awareness. We become mindful of eating both as a means of understanding and of mercifully meeting greater cravings. We unconditionally open to the long-conditioned. We no longer judge desire, or even hunger for it to desist, but simply meet with mercy these often merciless inclinations.

Traditionally the hungry ghost is often personified as having a gigantic mouth into which to stuff its enormous appetites. But a pencil-thin neck, and a throat so narrow nothing can be swallowed down. It has the bloated belly of the starving. Nothing of the outer world satisfies anything within. The ghost (the dense body) can somehow taste the world but is never nourished by it. It is very much like the stomach—it wishes to turn the whole world into itself. It lives outwardly in the senses, grasping at temporary satisfaction, never experiencing the ever-shining essence of being which is "pure satisfaction." It reads the menu by the light that comes from just beyond its appetites and dense longings.

There is a story from the Sufi tradition about the crazy wisdom figure Nasruddin, coming back from the market with a huge basket of hot peppers. Eating one after another, his tongue burning, his eyes watering, his nose running, he is asked by a student why he continues to abuse himself with these obviously burning morsels. Nasruddin looked up with a watery smile. "I keep looking for a sweet one!"

Does that sound familiar? Is it our "looking for a sweet one" that leaves that bitter taste? How much pain can we stand? How long do we, wishing only for a sweet one, continue to burn ourselves? And when do we discover we are the sweet one we are looking for, that we are looking for what is looking?

Becoming mindful of the process of eating we can explore this deep longing, the craving that leaves us so often unsated. Like any mechanical activity, when aware-ness of the process (mindfulness), is present, that which is usually below the level of awareness (creating involuntary activity) is brought into the light of a clear seeing. Where there is awareness, conditioning no longer acts on its own. The involuntary momentum is broken.

Mindfulness allows us to slow the moment, to be present during activities from which we are usually absent. No longer seduced into unconsciousness by unexplored desires for a "sweet one" and the fears which burn.

In a simpler time (of being) when hunger arose, we ate. But now, tangled in our personal history, cross-stimuli condition old reactions. We eat our grief. Fear arises and we chew harder. Doubt arises and we turn away from ourselves and face the refrigerator.

Ironically, the quality that motivates overeating—a wish to be satisfied, to be whole—is the same stimuli that propels deep spiritual inquiry. The hunger that leads to the dinner table leads to the meditation cushion as well. But hunger of a somewhat different sort. Hunger for wisdom, hunger for freedom, hunger for peace. This is the Great Desire which surrenders all lesser desires to the fire of investigation and letting go.

The Great Desire eats our pain and feeds the heart.

Ramana Maharshi spoke of tending the fire of freedom into which he surrendered his lesser desires, his smaller hungers, stirring the blaze with "the great staff of the Great Hunger for liberation." It is by the Great Desire (which can create the "nightmare of enlightenment," if unexplored) that we navigate through the pain of even that deep longing (longing creates suffering, not what is longed for) to the deep luminescence within. The light is attracted to the light.

The desire which leads to the dinner table creates more of the same. The desire of the meditation cushion creates less. The first attempts to feed the "I" of the "I am." It stands and hides while it eats. It thinks of itself as the body. The other is nurtured by the am-ness of the heart.

As one fellow said, who had been working with the eating meditation for some time, "The mouth is the mind in drag. It is an open tunnel to the roof of the skull and the hungry ghosts that hover there."

Taking our life back from the past we live step by step in the present. Feeling the miracle of the ground coming up to meet our feet so that we can, as Black Elk suggests, "walk in a sacred manner." We take each breath with the awareness of the body it nurtures and the miracle of the lightness of awareness within the denseness of form. "To breathe in a sacred manner." To honor even the hundreds of microbes that expire with each breath we take. Life eats life. We are all on the plate. All that lives is supported by the life of others. To live respectful of this process. To taste each mouthful of food. To breathe each breath. To live a moment at a time. "To eat in a sacred manner."

But first we learn to take a single bite. To be present a moment at a time. To see, smell, hear, feel, taste, and think one bite at a time. Opening to the instant in which life occurs. Not thinking our life or dreaming it. But directly experiencing it from instant to instant. Letting go of the moment passed, receiving each new arising. Drinking from the cup, not appraising it. Experiencing it directly not turning it to old mind, by adding just a pinch of memory and personal history, dreaming the parched dream, intensifying thirst.

Drinking from the cup—
Cool water
Thinking as I drink—
Stale memories
Mindful of thoughts—
Cool water.

Learning first to take a single bite we learn eventually to eat wholeheartedly. Aware not just of the eating but of the eater and the eaten as well. And the interconnected nature of each. Awakening to the true nature of eating, we uncover the true nature of the eater.

Eating is one of our favorite compulsive activities. Few meals eaten in a lifetime are thoroughly experienced.

Mindfulness of eating can deepen and broaden to a mindfulness of speech, of thought, of action, of intention. It allows the heart.

It is rumored that Jesus said, "Don't worry about what goes into your mouth, worry about what comes out of it!" Clarity comes not from *what* we put into our mouths, but from *how* we put it into our mouths. Just as it isn't what we do that liberates so much as how we do it. As one fellow puts it, "It's not how to do good, it's how to do good well."

Many people concerned with health or weight are thoughtful about what they eat but the real problem is how we eat. We eat on automatic. A forkful of food dropped into the mouth while still being chewed as it is approached with another forkful waiting like a dump truck to empty its contents and be on its way for the next haul. We chew facing a full fork, leaning into the next moment in order to consume more. We chew without tasting. We swallow with little awareness of our intention to swallow. We hardly see the food except on its first appearance, we hardly smell the food except on first approach. We hardly touch the food or sense its textures and consistency except on first consumption and even then only for a split second or two. We seldom feel the utensil in our hand. We seldom hear the utensil scraping the plate or the food crunched on the teeth. We are seldom aware of the tongue's activity moving the food about for equal distribution on the grinders.

Indeed, we sometimes wonder what that bitter after-taste is: it is sour grapes. A rationalization for another meal eaten but untasted. We miss so many meals, many feel as though they are starving.

Eating meditations are a part of many spiritual technol-ogies. They are a means of bringing the most ordinary and automatic of actions within a realm of healing awareness. And the possibility of what is called "free choice." When mindfulness is brought to the moment, we are able to respond from the appropriate rather than the automatic and old. To break the old in a moment of awareness is to live a moment anew. To meet the moment as it is arising is to be present in a merciful awareness which acts for the benefit of all, including ourselves.

There are various ways to approach lightly the compul-sive activity around eating and bring a new awareness to old hungers. Little mindfulnesses that stop reinforcing compulsive forgetfulness: to begin with, do not eat stand-ing. Sit to eat and first feel your body in the chair. Bring yourself wholeheartedly to the dinner table. To break automatic behavior you might also switch the eating utensil to the opposite hand. If you are right-handed, eat with your fork or chopsticks in the left hand; this will stop the automatic "shovel action." And watch yourself. When desire overcomes mindfulness, the fork flies, as if by magic, to the usual hand.

In eating, as in the rest of our lives, we attend to one thing at a time. When eating, we minimize distractions by eliminating any split in our attention such as music, television, other sensory inputs that might dull the focus on the process at hand. To do one thing at a time increases concentration and mindfulness throughout the day. Eating is the perfect opportunity to practice this single step at a time, this sacred manner in which to honor and live our lives. In keeping with this suggestion one might remember to put the fork down after the food is deposited in the mouth. While chewing, the fork can rest on the plate. As you put the fork down, notice the fingers hesitant to release the addiction to instant gratification.

Each time a forkful is raised to the mouth and empties its content therein, return that implement to the plate and let your hand rest softly beside it. Return your attention to the mouth, to the process of chewing, to the tongue arranging the food on the molars. To the process of tasting. Noticing any longing for a "sweet one." To the process of further mastication. To the process that follows the intention to swallow. To swallowing. To the intention to "get more." Taking a single bite we learn to eat in a sacred manner. Taking a single bite the whole meal is eaten moment to moment. Taking a single bite we open our heart not just our mouth.

By watching intention after intention, the compulsion to acquire more pleasant sensation, we see the basis of all our addictions.

Seeing how desire precedes intention, just as intention precedes action, we learn how to keep falling from moment to moment with little awareness of the life we think we lead but which actually leads us. Watching intention we break the automatic link between desire and action.

Tasting the food thoroughly, mindfully, we receive

delight without urgency. A mindful receiving of pleasure without a grasping at more or a fear of less. Then the agony within ecstasy is dissolved. Experiencing a single mouthful as taste, as touch, as fragrance, we are more deeply sated in the moment, belying our urgency for "more."

When this moment is enough, life is enough. When this moment isn't enough, nothing is enough.

One thing at a time. As in walking meditation or breathing meditation, we learn to take our first steps, our first breaths, and to live anew. So in eating meditation we learn to take a single bite and in that discover how to eat, how to live, in a sacred manner.

TAKING
A SINGLE BITE
MEDITATION

(To be read slowly to a friend or silently to oneself.)

Sit comfortably in your chair. Pull it up to the table. Feel how the chair supports you.

And feel this body that rests on this chair.

Notice sensations of pressure where the buttocks meet the chair. The pull of gravity.

Sensations in the body where the feet touch the floor.

Feel this body you sit in, this body you are about to nourish.

Feel the whole body as it is.

Sensations in the stomach perhaps.

Expectation at the tongue.

Desire in the mind.

Feel what comes now to eat.

And begin to soften the belly.

To let go of the tension, the expectation, the need that comes to the table disguised as appetite and preference.

Slowly allow the body to soften and open to receive sustenance.

Watch how even the expectation of pleasure can tighten the belly unpleasantly.

And soften once again.

The whole mind/body is involved in this process.

The sensations of being in a body received and acknowledged.

Now look at the table and the place setting before you.

See the plate before you and the food offered on that plate.

Notice how quickly thought names everything on the plate.

And how preference and desire immediately follow.

The food has already jumped off the plate into the mind.

The real thing once again exchanged for an idea, a bubble, a thought.

The living suchness of the food transformed to old mind so that what is eaten is seldom freshly tasted.

And once again we eat the same old meal, the same old way.

But awareness makes everything new, fresh, alive, in the moment. We are learning to be alive when eating.

We are learning to take a single bite.

As the mind observes the food, watch its reaction.

Notice any sense of urgency to get that food from the plate to the mouth. Soften the belly once again to receive nourishment, to be fully alive.

Notice the intention to reach for the fork.

As the hand extends toward the fork, feel the muscles in the arm, in the wrist, in the palm of the hand. Feel the movement instigated by intention, driven by desire.

Feel the hand open to lift the fork.

Notice the muscles in the palm of the hand.

Feel the slow extension of the fingers as they reach for the utensil.

Feel the cold of the fork when it is first touched.

Lifting the fork, notice the extensors and contractors in the arm which allow the hand its perfect navigation toward the mouth. The hand-eye coordination of fulfillment.

As the sense of smell arises, notice the fragrance of food entering the nostrils. Breathe it deeply into the body. Participate in smelling.

Notice how smelling is the taste that precedes chewing and the swallowing.

Feel the fork as it lifts the food.

Forearm swinging back, the elbow pulling toward the body to leverage the awaited food toward the waiting mouth.

Notice the sensations in the jaw.

Watch how the tongue extends anxiously to receive sensation.

Feel the touch of the fork as it brushes the lips.

Notice the touch of the food on the tongue.

Sensation in the body; expectation in the mind.

Feel the food on the tongue.

Notice the first burst of pleasure as tasting arises.

Observe the mouth closing as it prepares to chew, the muscles in the jaw contracting, the sensations of teeth coming in contact with food.

Chewing. Taste arising.

Chewing.

Taste arising.

Notice how the tongue moves the food around in the mouth for better leverage.

Notice how the teeth have stopped their movement for just a moment to receive more food.

Put the fork down.

While chewing, just chew.

Not chewing and shoveling and choosing and chewing some more.

Not swallowing lumps of food, one after another.

Just one mouthful at a time.

Take a single bite wholeheartedly.

As other desires rise for other flavors, notice the quality of liking and disliking with each moment of taste, of texture, of change.

Notice the quality of texture in the food changing from the first bite to the next—from a solid to a mush—changing again and again.

Notice how the food comes to equal consistency and how quickly the intention to swallow follows automatically.

Notice the intention to swallow.

See how desire creates an intention to fulfill desire and how action arises from such an intention.

Watch the reflexes necessary as the food moves to the back of the mouth and down the funnel toward the stomach.

Don't get lost searching for more satisfaction. Stay with the sensations of eating, of chewing, of swallowing.

Feel the food descend past the heart into the deep softness of the belly.

Is the fork back in the hand, poised with another mouthful? How did it get there?

Return the fork to the plate and take the hand away as chewing occurs.

Taking a single bite, all the senses are employed.

See the food, its colors, its form outlined against the plate.

Smelling, inhaling taste as fragrance.

Feeling the whole body engaged in the process.

Being present in the present.

Each time a forkful or spoonful is raised to the mouth and empties its contents therein, return that implement to the plate.

Lay your hand softly beside it and return your attention to the mouth, to the body, to the mind. Exploring, experiencing directly, the wide range of feelings and sensations in the process of eating.

Watching the tendency of the hungry mind to lean into the next moment—to seek imagined satisfaction in some imagined future—we recognize that desire for "more" so clearly while eating. And we touch with mercy that profound longing for completion and satisfaction.

Returning your attention to the mouth, to the process of chewing, to the tongue adjusting the food, to the process of tasting, masticating, swallowing.

Swallowing mindfully.

Eating the whole meal a bite at a time.

Taking a single bite, we eat in a sacred manner.

Taking a single bite, the whole meal is honored moment to moment.

Taking a single bite, life becomes the banquet.

A FURTHER INQUIRY
INTO EATING

One Zen master said that eating was "putting nothing into nothing." What a banquet to partake of the all-inclusive vastness which "contains" nothing though it is perceivable in everything. God putting God into God. And in this vastness there is not even "nothing." As indescribable as uncontained space. Sacred emptiness. Limitless. Unable to be touched but often felt. Unable to be tasted yet ever so tasty. Seldom able to be heard until it is drawn through the mind of a Mozart or a Rumi or a thrush. It is the sound of the wind in the trees. It is also the sound of the trees when no wind blows. In listening, we hear. In tasting, we get the flavor of the unlimited, our true nature. Inhaling its fragrance causes us almost to swoon. In thinking it is seeing thought as process and we dissolve into that space in which the process floats. No watcher, no watched. No eater, no eaten. Just the eating itself. Just process unfolding in the sharp focus of a luminescent awareness. Just the watching unfolding in the vastness. Sharing, not owning, the life force within all that is. A part of the great interconnectedness of all things.

"More" is not enough. Only the One (our shared suchness) will do. The rest is restlessness.

Just as intention propels desire into action like a drive shaft which conveys the thrust of the motor to the spinning wheels, so the fork connects the food seen and smelled on the plate with the hungry mouth of longed-for satisfaction.

To eat mindfully we need develop a mindful relationship with the fork.

See it. Feel it. Pick it up. Load it. Pull it toward the mouth. Notice its feel on lips or tongue. Notice it go back to the plate all by itself. Watch it wait impatiently to dump its load and hurry off for more. Watch it troll for satisfaction on the plate selecting the next morsel. And up like a steam shovel toward the mouth. In *The Fork Story* is every play by Shakespeare, every poem by Baudelaire or Poe, every country love song.

Forks can eat by themselves. They must be watched. Know your fork!!!

THE FORK STORY

Everyone knows all too well the infamous Fork Story *and the compulsion it personifies:*

Watch it lie casually on the table. A metal sculpture. A solid object. It casts shadows.

This object is not so innocent as its momentary immobility suggests. It is an obvious implement of attack, a machine of the senses.

Notice it cool to the first touch. And how quickly it warms in the hungry grasp. Soon it becomes invisible to the hand, an extension of the desire body.

Watch it load itself up for the hoist to the tongue. Full of broccoli and expectation.

And the rush toward the senses, mouth agape. As the stomach grunts, "Give me eat!"

The tongue, a good deal more sophisticated than "that animal, the stomach," flattens like a supplicant in full prostration to acquire that first mouthful.

Then flips it back toward the ready grinders that release the first rush of flavor.

Taste after taste unfolds. Textures changing and changing again.

The fork long since gone and returned, waiting just beyond the lips "for another hit."

The tongue has not even finished its swirling and tasting before the desire for "more" causes us involuntarily to swallow. Though the tongue curls back, almost jumping down the throat after the disappearing food, wanting "just one more taste."

But the lips remember, as the panic diminishes, that another forkload is but a moment away. And the jaw unhinges like a baby bird's beak to receive "the next delicious morsel."

Tongue slightly extended, anxious for the next moment to occur.

The mind full of liking and disliking, mouthful to mouthful, chew to chew, taste to taste, moment to moment.

And desire abates for just a moment at the center of a certain taste or texture as we experience "satisfaction."

But then the wish for "more" rearises. The hungry ghosts reassert themselves all by themselves and the clear waters of the mind once again become agitated by longing. That which was an object of satisfaction a moment before becomes "something to protect," something to lose. More grief. The swirling waters of expectation and dissatisfac-

tion, unfulfilled and longing for the satisfaction which lies just beneath our longing.

And again the fork tells us to eat our grief. Cleverly it corrals the peas in cream sauce and herds them toward the mashed potatoes. The stomach full, but the tongue still craving as the final morsel is devoured. Watchfulness has long since pushed itself full-bellied from the table and gone off for a snooze as the fork unconsciously finishes its appointed rounds.

But remembering once again that we are alive, we explore the moment. We take a single bite in a sacred manner and gradually we are freed from the "emergency of desire," that panicky longing which creates such grief. Mindfulness of eating. Awareness heals.

Through direct seeing, one sees clearly, experiencing not just what is seen but the mechanics of seeing as well. So one learns to hear, taste, feel, smell, and think directly and clearly in the moment. It is a direct entering into "reality," examining and penetrating the veils of long-conditioned perception that blur the senses and fill the mind with ghostly images of the old. It wakes us from the recapitulated dream.

Entering directly our lives, not seeing the same old sight in the same old way (mind), or tasting the same old meal (mind), or smelling the same old fragrance (mind), or thinking the same old thought (mind), one no longer reacts to stimuli but learns to respond. To enjoy so much more deeply the newness of each bite, of each breath, of each step. Caught less in deeply conditioned ways of experiencing and interpreting the moment past.

Mindfulness dissolves death and the deadness in our lives by taking us into the sacred present.

And then what?
A Zen master might say, "Wash the dishes."
Enlightenment does not stop with the last forkful.

Clear the senses as you clean the dishes. Notice the warmth of the water. The texture of the slippery soap film on the plate. Notice any intention to rush. Or to think that essential satisfaction is to be found anywhere else.

Clean the silverware last. Honor your tools. Polish your fork thoroughly, mindfully, and in a sacred manner.

This is the zen of the fork.

But eating does not end with cleaning your dish. Later as you sit mindfully on the commode, be aware of the aftermath of digestion—the processing by the body of those mashed potatoes and gravy, and obviously the corn. And notice the vibrating body you sit in.

Excrete with gratitude and awareness.

This is the zen of the bathroom.

This is not the end of The Fork Story.

TO EAT IN A SACRED MANNER

To eat in a sacred manner is to be conscious of the interconnected nature of the eaten and the eater. To honor the eaten. To be aware of what the exceptional teacher Thich Nhat Hanh refers to as "interbeing."

To eat in a sacred manner we need to learn to eat from the heart. Thus we begin with the soft-belly meditation, which allows us to loosen the long-held grief that tightens the belly. Touching with mercy and awareness the pain that imprisons the stomach deep in hard belly, we free the stomach to take nourishment at last. And we attend to each element of this sacred process.

When we eat in a sacred manner, the body is fed for survival and service. Eating doesn't stop at the tongue. We offer sustenance to the whole body, received in soft belly. We honor the process of life and the lineage of creatures sacrificed to the plate. We eat for the benefit of all sentient beings.

We develop this sense of interconnectedness by acknowledging all that is eaten in its original form: envisioning the wheat that comprises the bread, the milk of the cow, the pod of the pea. The ocean of fish. And the sun which feeds them all. We take in the sacred, the germ of life, like the Eucharist, in gratitude and respect.

When we learn to eat from the heart we honor the stomach, not just the tongue. We are once again like children learning haltingly to feed ourselves, to nurture deep hungers in a way that heals painful longings rather than intensifies them. When we eat from just the tongue a single organ overrides the "good sense" of all the other senses. To be led by a single organ to the detriment of all other gives insight into other compulsiveness as well.

To eat in a sacred manner is to eat mindful of the sacred, the one life we all share. To eat in a sacred manner is to attend directly to the underlying divinity of all that eats and is eaten.

When we eat in a sacred manner we are no longer the cause of world hunger but a possible solution. As we partake mindfully of the lives of others, focused on the shared essence, a sudden wordless understanding arises—we sense the inseparableness of all that is. We sense the depth of the truth that Buddha transmitted when he said that if we knew the enormous power that giving has to tune us in to our shared essence, we would offer to others a part of every meal eaten. When you eat in a sacred manner you never eat alone. When you eat in a sacred manner each meal is preceded by a prayer for the well-being of all those who go to bed hungry tonight. We remember the face of that homeless child on the streets of New York City when asked, "Do you get enough to eat?" And his reply, "Sometimes I get crazy hungry!" To eat in a sacred manner is to serve the world.

And on a blatantly personal note, if you will excuse the hypocrisy and conceit of opinion—if one wants to end starvation in the world, one might consider lessening the consumption of meat for which the rain forests are being depleted and the greenhouse effect exacerbated. And to which hundreds of thousands of acres of fertile land, which could feed millions, is sacrificed to the appetites of a relative few. It is an egregious waste of resources. But beyond these mental flurries there is a matter of the heart. Indeed, it's not a question of meat or meat eating but just the simple fact of the unnecessary suffering of our fellow beasts. (See John Robbins' *Diet for a New America*.)

To eat in a sacred manner is to learn to eat the moment directly, as it occurs, not as a vague aftertaste we lament on our deathbed.

On his deathbed a Zen master was brought his favorite pastry by a student who asked, "What is the nature of life, of death?" To which the old man replied, "My but this cake is delicious!" He ate in a sacred manner. He died in a sacred manner.

A GUIDED MEDITATION FOR EATING IN A SACRED MANNER

(To be read slowly to a friend or silently to oneself.)

As you approach the table reflect on the death-defying act of eating.

Sit in your chair and feel the chair beneath the buttocks. Feel its support against the back.

Feel this body sitting there.

Be aware of the body in its relationship to the table and the food on the plate. Body awareness.

Honor the food on the plate. Notice the shapes of the food, its color. Notice how color defines form. How the green curve of a pea against the white plate delineates its roundness. Learning to see how to see.

Having examined the food in its present form, envision the food in its original condition. In the bread, golden fields of wheat waving in the wind. Mountain streams. Eggs in a nest. The black and white Guernsey which offered the milk. The green peas nestled in pods on flowing vines. The dark earth. The rain. And always the sun. Rice paddies. Bean stalks. Potatoes dug by strong hands from the ground.

160

And if there is meat on the plate, see the animal from which it came. The cows in the field, or in trucks shipped to market. The herds of docile sheep. The snorting swine. The silent fish.

Then picture yourself gathering the food—perhaps singing or chanting to the life about to be consumed. See yourself picking the asparagus, selecting tomatoes from the plant, cutting the wheat or grain, sorting herbs or spices. And if there is meat, picture that animal. Sing to her. Praise him. Send gratitude for the flesh offered.

This is an envisioning, with the heart's eye, of the food which is to be consumed.

Honoring the origins of the food, focus on the environment in which the food is to be consumed. The table, the tablecloth, the design on the plate. The levels in the salt and pepper shakers. The slight curve of liquid as it adheres to the edges of the glass.

Bless the food on the plate. See each mouthful as if it were one more breath, allowing life to remain in the body a moment longer. Thank it. Use it well. Inhale its aroma. Notice how the fragrance of food is devoured in the nostrils. Savour directly the separate aromas. Attend to how the aroma of the steaming peas smells differently from that of the baked potato. Watch how fragrance stimulates desire. Fragrance is foreplay. Learning to smell.

Observe how desire comes rapidly to the surface from a sideways glance, a momentary sniff, a passing memory.

Inhaling mindfully. Exhaling mindfully.

Reaching for a utensil, the muscles in the arm, the extensors and contractors, are experienced directly as they respond to the intention to pick up the fork, the knife, the chopsticks. Honoring the weight of the fork in the hand. Feel its roughness. Its smoothness. Its coldness. Its increasing warmth. Watch these sensations constantly changing. Learning to touch.

Contact directly the sensations arising from the utensil felt in the hand.

Having noticed the intention to pick up the fork, and feeling the fork thoroughly in the hand, in the fingers, attend to the muscles of the forearm and biceps as the fork arcs toward the plate.

Sacred presence in a body at a table.

Feel the tip of the fork angling for food and the slight change in weight as the food is raised from the plate.

Sensations flowing from the plate toward the mouth.

Investigating the cold of the fork as it touches the lips. Feel the jaw swing open to expose the oral cavity to food. Direct touching.

Hearing the fork as it scrapes against the plate, notice too the birds in the trees, the wind in the branches. The noise in the street, the voice in the mind. Learning to hear.

Feel the food on the tongue. Direct sensation.

Notice the intention of the mouth to close.

Tasting the food on the tongue. Honor its various textures and how they change with mastication. Notice the elements of sweetness or sourness, bitterness or spice, that comprise each moment of tasting. Noticing moment to moment the ever-changing quality of flavor. Learning to taste.

Notice any automatic or mechanical quality in the chewing process. Slowing down, tasting thoroughly. Tasting directly.

Honoring the mind's response to the food, notice how automatically liking and disliking arises from bite to bite.

How liking leads to longing.

How longing energizes expectation.

How expectation fears dissatisfaction.

How that fear of "less" propels intention.

How intention crafts response.

How response becomes lost in reaction.

How reacting, we act in the same old way.

See how mindfulness of the sacred stops the conspiracy.

Honoring this ancient momentum, we do not meet it with judgement but with mercy and respect. Watch the chain of events in the mind as passing show.

Notice how each moment conditions the next.

Honoring the process floating in sacred emptiness.

Observe desire's relationship to food. The drive toward gratification. The leaning toward more. Observe directly the mind. Learn to think. Learn to feel.

In each mouthful opportunities for the sacred. For sacred touching. For sacred hearing. For sacred smelling. For sacred thinking. For sacred feeling.

And in the heart such gratitude for this moment of life, this sacred morsel.

ANOTHER SACRED BITE

When we eat in a sacred manner, even if the meal is disappointing—overcooked, too much sauce, lima beans—we have an opportunity for healing insight.

When we enter our longing in a sacred manner, in mercy and awareness, the whole meal is eaten in the heart of the divine. Each moment frees the last. That which had devoured the world, that which fed our hunger, realigns and begins to feed the hungry.

When we eat in a sacred manner, honoring one bite at a time, we turn hell to heaven. We take our lives out of the shadows of the old into the luminescence of the new. Discovering the floating presence in the present. Honoring being.

As eating becomes a prayer for the benefit of all that is sacred—all that lives and breathes, all that, just as ourselves, wishes only to be happy—a sense of the sacred pervades our life. Entering the one life we all share we become the sacred. Eating then becomes just a process of letting the unnameable immensity receive the world in mercy and peace.

When we eat in a sacred manner there is not someone eating something, there is only being partaking of itself. There is just a certain joy unfolding.

To bring the unconscious within consciousness is to honor our own life and the lives of all who nourish us. It breaks the momentum of unseen tendencies before they act themselves out. To unlock a single sense or appetite is to have access to the whole field of desire.

Noting with soft belly the dense clouds of desire which obscure the luminescence of our true nature, we go beyond the self-conscious "me," which always eats alone no matter how great the feast. To break this same old way of eating, the same old meal forever, is to sense the divinity of the eaten and the eater, to participate directly in the eating itself. Thus we take a single bite in order to honor the whole world and to eat and walk and live in a sacred manner.

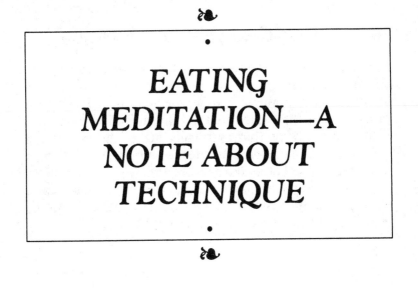

EATING MEDITATION—A NOTE ABOUT TECHNIQUE

Eating is an active meditation. Active practices have a special benefit. When active practices are well-developed they become what is called in some Zen monasteries "work meditation." It is being not lost in doing.

In the case of the active practice of the eating meditations (and certainly with all the meditations enclosed) there is a process in making them one's own.

Because these guided eating meditations cannot be used in the beginning with the eyes closed, one must first learn the technique before undertaking the practice. So the meditation is first approached as a contemplation. It is read and reread, closing the eyes now and then to absorb the previous paragraph.

The meditations can then be read or listened to on tape while eating a few raisins or peanuts or perhaps a few of each alternately in order to explore changes in texture, flavor, preference, intention. (When you eat and listen, *only* eat and listen.)

Eventually, however, like all meditation, it is not read or listened to but internalized through attentive repetition. This is the process that eventually makes the meditation your own. Then one *becomes* the meditation, it is no longer just a technique but a change in lifestyle.

This is precisely how working, with some continuity, with the Taking a Single Bite meditation evolves naturally into the practice of Eating in a Sacred Manner.

•

EATING PLAY
An Experiment in Consciousness

•

Eat the same thing each day for a week. Watch how desire relates to not getting what it wants.

As a means of playing lightly with even heavier states, it is valuable to explore such basic needs and primal peevishness as are embroiled in the sense of taste. There are few areas where we can so readily see the desire for "more" as when we are eating and selecting flavors.

There are a few ways one can play with this eating inquiry. For one, select a food that offers balanced nutrition, such as rice and beans, and eat only that for a week or a month—the length of time depending on your interest in such investigation.

Another way is simply to choose the same foods for each of the three meals during the day, perhaps eating only oatmeal for each breakfast, a sandwich for each lunch, and rice and beans for supper. Continue to eat these same foods for a week. Watch the mind's tendencies and querulousness at not getting just what it wants. Note the sadness that accompanies our holding to things being different. Note the joy at letting go into what is.

If you want to increase the intensity of this practice, commit to holding the utensil in the hand opposite the one you usually use. Doing so will break some of the unconscious momentum of desire manifesting itself in action. It will also give some insight into the volitional quality that precedes each action as we notice again and again the unrequested intention to switch the utensil to the easier modality.

Insight arises when we bring the nearly involuntary drive of desire into mindfulness. Attending carefully to each incremental moment of the fulfillment of desire, we see that desire has a life of its own and its own personal history. Then we do not so much declare war on desire and attempt to *force* desirelessness (motivated by the desire to remove the unpleasant) but begin instead to make peace with our longings.

When desire is no longer an object of judgement but is recognized as the cause of so much suffering in ourselves and the world, the merciful investigation of desire settles into the heart as a lifelong healing practice. When we let the Great Desire eat all other desires, we are never hungry.

Someone asked, "Why eat the same thing everyday?"

Because you didn't taste it the last time!

WHEN BUDDHISTS MEDITATE

When human beings meditate
they sometimes close their eyes
and feel this body—
a flickering field of sensations—
a tingling, hot and cold,
gravity here and there.

And attend to the breath
at the belly or nostrils
choose one
and stay there five years—

not the thought of the breath
but the sensations accompanying
each inhalation
each exhalation.

169

The beginning
the middle
the end
of each in-breath
and the space between
where thinking wriggles free.

The beginning
middle
and end
of each out-breath

and the space between
and thought
and the space between thoughts

returning to the breath—
just sensation breathing itself.
Sensations sensing themselves
floating in space.

Even some idea of who
is doing all this
floats by
just another bubble

another thought thinking itself
mirroring like Escher
the fragile moment
vanishing in space

returning to the breath like a devotee
who has broken vows
a thousand times
and returns unruffled
once again.

Watching thoughts
think themselves
one into the next—
beginning momentarily to exist
and dissolving—
even such notions as impermanence
pass in the flow.

Observing feeling arise
uninvited—
unexpectedly impersonal
no one to blame
or be blamed only
rope burns from grasping
at change.

And return to the breath again
awareness making the old
brand new.

Watching consciousness dream
self and the world—
constantly creating more
of there less to be.

Observing content dying
into process
floating in space.

We seek only to discover
that what is sought
leaves the seeker far behind.

We are what we are looking for,
for lack of a larger term,
God.

REMEMBERING

Much of practice is a simple remembering. Remembering the breath, remembering to be mindful, remembering our true nature, and remembering the space it is all floating in.

In remembering there is a momentary pause in which the light may enter the process.

Often the difference between bondage and freedom, between being lost in dense mental states and rediscovering the space in which they float, is simply remembering the belly or the breath. Or it may be a simple noting of the moment. Simply focusing. A merciful awareness.

To help us share this teaching with workshop participants, we had for many years a large banner which read REMEMBER. We would sometimes hang the banner on the wall behind us when we taught. But we stopped bringing the banner to workshops because I kept leaving it behind.

Clearly here was a teaching for me; a reminder to remember.

Some days I remember with the first breath. Some days not until I see Maharaji's eyes or Ondrea's. But when the heart is present, even if I don't remember, I never forget.

TAKE IT LIGHTLY

A better term than enlightenment is simply lightenment.

Let go of enlightenment lightly. There is no goal. There is only process. There are no losers.

The concept of enlightenment closes hearts and tightens sphincters for most "aspirants." Many use it as a form of self-flagellation. It strikes against the deep "not enoughness" that the mind is so wont to produce when forced to become.

Peak experience is to the mind what orgasm is to the body, and both are subject to considerable performance anxiety.

The concept of enlightenment (as opposed to its actuality) turns our everyday grief to a daily suffering. We dig in for the leap of faith as though it were a footrace. Enlightenment is our birthright. Lightenment is the process. A gradual letting go. A deeper letting be. A broader healing.

It is play and heartful nonsense. A healing wisdom, a bit more clarity, a bit more love.

Ironically even classic "enlightenment" experiences may ultimately do more to lighten than enlighten. Six months after such peak experiences, even for advanced meditators, they may be clearer and lighter—but still certain latent tendencies might remain.

It is said that enlightenment takes from thirty years to a millisecond—usually both. Why are you scowling? How much grief demands to be erased? And with how much mercy can we now meet this pain that longs for future enlightenment?

EXPLORING THE REAL BODY

A Zen master once told a friend who had mentioned he did "service work" with schizophrenic teenagers that the only service you can do for another is to reinforce trust in their real nature!

To teach techniques for deep inquiry and self-discovery is the greatest service we can do anyone. To share the joy of our underlying reality, our true nature, the unlimited Real Body. Then no matter what we are doing we will constantly be expanding the context in which it is happening. And there will be so much more space to let go into.

When the Real Body is our context, illness in our dense body is not an emergency but rather a teaching. And we relate to illness not as punishment or some indication of previous holding, but as an exquisite opportunity to enter directly our deepest healing. Then illness or injury reminds us of the ever uninjured and uninjurable quality of our true

176

nature, and we continue expanding into the healing that goes beyond cure.

When the context is "my body" then it's *my* pain and *my* illness and *my* difficulty at healing. All is struggle and failure. But when the context is "*the* body," a sense of the universal enters *the* pain, and healing becomes the space in which the unhealed floats.

The Real Body is the body of awareness. It is the deathless, the boundaryless spaciousness of being. Edgeless awareness.

The Real Body is the unborn. It is the most of us.

The Real Body can be discovered exploring directly the flickering body and mind of our temporary birth. The Real Body is not about time or space. Indeed, duration and loss have nothing to do with it. It is the vibrating suchness of being, out of which consciousness and all worlds manifest while it examines how many electrons can spin on the head of a pin.

When Krishna whispered this secret to Buddha, the gods became just more stars in a cluttered sky and he laughed like lightning in the clouds and rained for forty days just to clear his throat.

The Real Body is the primordial body, the body before form. It precedes even the light body and subtle astral bodies that so many seekers speak of in their travelogues. Indeed, the light of the light body is the energy emitted when the formlessness bursts into form. Before even these subtler bodies manifest from subtler attachments to form. What we call "our body," the flickering body, is born from the Real Body. A bit of previous momentum.

The Real Body is not this pleasured and pained, tight-bellied, born-and-dying flesh. It is the body of beingness. To this enormity the flickering body is but a slight protuberance toward the surface, a minor universe.

The long-conditioned mind makes small bodies and huge limitations. The heart makes nothing. It needs nothing. Following the essence of awareness and loving kindness which arises spontaneously from the *"uh"* of being, we take its cues to hold nowhere and proceed lightly through the ten thousand realms of the mind to the light which lies beyond.

The Zens ask, "What was your face before you were born?" What is the unchanging *"uh"* of being, the only constant in life? What is that in which all these impermanent thoughts of who we are, or might be, float and flicker? Does this *"uh,"* by which we surmise we exist, seem to have a beginning and an end? Or is it just *the* beingness out of which *our* beingness arises?

Krishna, between the battle lines of the conflicted mind, turns to Arjuna and tells him to see the mind and body from the vantage point of "the real."

Never the spirit was born;
the spirit shall cease to be never.
Never was time it was not;
End and beginning are dreams
birthless and deathless,
and changeless
remaineth the spirit forever;
death hath not touched it at all
dead though the house of it seems.

If you think you are *this* flickering body you will become confused after death. Stop nowhere! All temporal protuberances dissolve, no matter how beautiful or frightening, no matter how subtle or gross. The Real Body is the mind before thinking, before "me and mine."

The mind, which concocts the "me" and "the world," is an atom on a short chain molecule. A particle on a single strand of DNA woven into a minuscule gene (or cosmos), lost in the enormous glitter of the shimmering double helix, extending like the milky way off into our Real Body.

FIRST SNOW

For this first amazing snow
I thank all the tiny Gods
Krishna, Athena, Jesus and Buddha
that float in my Real Body.

Even in our flickering body
somewhere toward the surface
there is a glistening
like the sun
reflected in a whirlpool.
It is the cycle of birth and death
a peripheral cosmos
a universe of possibilities.

The formless protrudes
into form—

the Big Bang
or the least thought
can do it.

Einstein recommended the meditation
at the edge where nothing
expands into "less than nothing"—
where content is invisible
and form depends on content.

Where the surface of the swirling worlds
evaporate into consciousness
there is a distant galaxy
dissolving
like these amazing snowflakes
imposturing reality—
unable to measure
the melting.

AN EXPLORATION
OF RESISTANCE

Resistance is an unwillingness to go further. It is a reaction (as opposed to response) to pain, mental or physical. Left uninvestigated, it stops us in our tracks.

When one begins to practice, and throughout one's spiritual life, there may be periods when it is difficult to meditate. Times of agitated restlessness and aversive boredom. Or the sluggish attachment to easier ways. Sometimes this restlessness is due to some old wound approaching the surface. Sometimes this restlessness is because of the fear that arises as we approach unexplored territory. Fear often accompanies growth because all growth happens at our edges—and a step beyond. Sometimes it is merely because we wish to be elsewhere "enjoying ourselves." Desire for the pleasant creating a tense unpleasantness. Sometimes it is the anxiety that accompanies our healing. Often it is simply an imbalance between our concentration and energy. When the concentration is greater than the energy present, we experience "sinking mind," a dull-eyed dreaminess. When the energy is greater than the concentration, we are left with a restlessness and difficulty staying present.

All of this may intensify the desire for things to be otherwise. This desire "for something different" is our resistance. Resistance is a desire not to be present.

Looking inward we find some difficulty making contact with areas that have long gone uninvestigated. There may be a "protective armoring" and a certain restlessness surrounding these long-isolated and often numbed areas of our aversion. It is the reason we didn't start sooner. This unwillingness seems unworkable to the thinking-fatigued mind. We may even doubt that the practice will "do it for us," and so, why bother!? This is our resistance to our resistance.

Exploring resistance teaches patience. Not waiting patiently for resistance to dissolve—for one is either waiting or one is patient. One is either leaning toward the next moment or present in each moment unfolding. To work with resistance, to investigate and see beyond, is to cultivate a merciful, choiceless, non-interfering awareness—just what is needed for what is coming.

Resistance refuses "just this much." When this occurs, rather than trying to get around the resistance, focus on it. Watch the fist of our fear closing down around "the uncontrollable," producing feelings of helplessness and dismay.

Many, when trying to watch the pain in the mind or the pain in the body, have some difficulty approaching and receiving directly the experience. They find it quite difficult to "just sit with it." Our long-conditioned resistance to the disagreeable tightens the mind and body. It is another unsuccessful jailbreak. An attempt at flight—like a tethered bird beating its wings against the fragile air, its body falling back again and again to the ground, fatigued and panicked. The attempt at flight is a greater suffering than the momentary tether was a pain.

When people come to us and say they are trying to approach their pain and heal it but "resistance keeps getting in the way," we encourage them to work with what is. "Don't try to get around the resistance, get into it. *Resistance is the meditation.*"

There is no rush. Rushing is just another form of resistance. Another impatience with what is. Another grumbling complaint blocking the throat of the "still small voice within."

Working with resistance, as with any discomfort, one approaches a step at a time. Working with the most obvious elements of that which turns pain into suffering, we open the heart to observe the mind's functions and dysfunctions with a gentle and merciful awareness.

As with any dense mental or physical pain, the meditation may be worked with ten or fifteen minutes at a time. Then take a break and go fully back to the breath for a while, softening the belly and watching the breath from that softness. By not attacking the area (resisting the moment), even in the slightest, we swing back to the healing or pain or resistance meditation for whatever period feels appropriate. While some areas of the body almost sing in the light of awareness, others may be difficult to contact directly. Patience furthers. If some sense of resistance or urgency predominates, gradually allow awareness to approach that area with a willingness to liberate this pained state of mind.

In order to enter directly this resistance, it may be necessary at first to use a visualization meditation. This may allow one to approach and make contact with resistance at levels not previously available. It is a powerful focus for the mind which has been withdrawn from its pain, and thus the world, by deeply conditioned resistance.

Although visualization is one step removed from the

direct experience of the area itself, its power to approach the center of what is happening and eventually reveal its inner contents to direct investigation can be very skillfully applied.

This is a path-clearing meditation. It allows one to directly approach the qualities that arise in the mind, which obscure the heart. The first hindrance seems always to be a hindering of our ability to relate directly to the hindrances themselves.

This technique of healing resistance is based on the recognition that to see clearly the nature of our grasping we need open our hands. Running for a bus or train, holding to our luggage "for all we're worth," when at last, we sink to our seat, we may find it difficult to open the hand back into its natural spaciousness. It has become clamped closed. We may even have to peel the fingers back one by one. This returning to openness may at times be a painful process. Our mind, like the hand of a sleeping baby, is by its original nature open and soft, but it has become rigor-mortised around desire and fear. Clearly desire and fear are not the problem. It is our identification and grasping that cause suffering. Letting go is the cure.

Those who find this hindrance at times limiting, but have both the capacity to go further and a sense of the power of visualization to open contact with an area, may find this practice useful. It is begun by envisioning a large hand closing around the qualities in the mind or body that the mind labels pain. It is the fist of our resistance. It is that which holds so, and closes down on discomfort. It is that which turns discomfort to pain and eventually pain to suffering.

If in the course of your inner process one finds oneself "up against the wall" because of dense mental or physical states, always, of course, the foundation of practice, mindfulness, is called for. But there are aids to mindfulness.

Specific focal points for dissolving hardened layers of holding, armoring, as one heals back into one's own life. One's own true nature. The use of "hindrance meditations" such as the resistance or heavy state investigation are a skillful means of going deeper by investigating the ground beneath our feet. Resistance keeps us from wholly touching that ground. When we surrender this holding in the great sigh of letting go, the earth comes up to support each step.

Trust in the process is the opposite of resistance. Without trust in the process we will always be relating from the pain rather than to it.

Not judging even judgement. Not closing even to our heart being closed. Not hiding in the armoring of hard belly. Healing spontaneously arises when we let go of holding to our resistance, looking with a merciful awareness on each unfolding in the mind/body.

In the course of looking inward, when resistance becomes evident, one can visualize this fist of resistance and slowly, with mercy and awareness, begin to open finger by finger, this long accumulated denseness. Surrendering finger by finger the suffering one has held to for so long.

Letting go of our suffering is the hardest work we will ever do.

Seeing the long-accumulated, long-reinforced, large-knuckled fist of our holding no longer as the "protector" but rather as the "jailer," we begin to soften the resistance which has imprisoned us in the old, superficial and rusted for so long. Seeing that which magnifies discomfort into inaccessible pain we begin to surrender finger by finger, moment by moment, the considerable tension around discomfort.

To test this truth, push against some pain with all your might and feel the extraordinary painfulness that arises. Now just take a few soft breaths and soften all around it— just let it float. How does that feel?

*Surrender is not defeat. It is a letting go of resistance.
It is opening to our pain. It is about ending our suffering.*

Begin by visualizing this resistance, this tense fist. Observe how it holds to the pain and obscures the heart. It fills the mind with agitation and added discomfort. A single moment of insight into how this grasping creates suffering can change our whole perspective. And offer insight into so much that causes difficulty and hindrance in our lives. The very ability to visualize it without any need to change it is already an aspect of our non-resistance to resistance. We are cultivating a willingness to approach that which has warned us off for so long. The heart's entrance into our pain. Indeed, we are learning to keep our hearts open in hell.

When the mind produces resistance, just having considered using the meditation means there already is a willingness to go beyond unwillingness and allow this state to float unresisted in awareness. So we slowly begin to release our holding around pain. To allow a sense of spaciousness into that area. To allow the healing in. Visualize that fist remembering to let go. Remembering its natural openness once again. Let it sigh. Let its tension be released as a new warmth and mercy flood the soft flesh of kindness and care. Moment-to-moment surrender, moment-to-moment letting go. The fingers softening and opening around the long-obscured and deeply numbed pains of our existence.

Discovering within the fist of our holding, the open-handed surrender to healing. The vast "don't know" which is vulnerable to miracles and the truth. We see the fist opening as though discovering a remarkable gift that lies gently in its palm; it is called "the wish-fulfilling gem." See it as the sacred hand of service letting go of that which limits healing.

In this visualization there can be a deep softening of the ligaments, the flesh, the musculature all around the place of suffering or discomfort to allow sensation to just be as it is. To float in something greater than old mind's insistent clinging.

This visualization, if skillfully applied, can lead to a greater spaciousness and openness that allows awareness to enter directly into the cosmos pulsing at the center of each sensation—each pain, each numbness, each distrusting womb, each aching heart and frightened mind, discovering that liberation is their birthright.

Observing, when a merciful awareness enters directly a heavy state of mind, how that state naturally disperses when there is nothing holding it back or impeding its natural impermanence, we discover the liberating power of awareness. And how loving kindness and mercy combined with deep awareness manifests as letting go.

Watching how love and awareness balance heavy states of mind, how fear, doubt, and anger obscure the heart of our wholeness, we get a sense of where our freedom may be found. We see how the pain of holding seems to float, then disintegrate, in the merciful light of a new clarity.

Indeed, if one could see deeply the nature of resistance, one would experience directly that which limits us to the closed, rusted, and dysfunctional. Opening to resistance, trust evolves where there was distrust before.

Resistance is the chapped fist that grasps the tiny fears we fear to let go of. We keep burying ourselves alive. Until we ever so slowly open that fist, letting go of the fear of the "uncontrollable moment." We let go thinking it is our fear that will float away, but it turns out it is "being afraid" that floats free even though fear may still be present.

When we let go of our pain we become the letting go, not the pain. We float free.

A friend stymied by unsuccessful attempts to elude his strong resistance to meditation and other pains eventually surrendered his pain into a graffiti scrawled on his kitchen wall.

Don't get around it
  Get into it—
    Get off it
  Get on with it!

A GUIDED VISUALIZATION ON RESISTANCE

(To be read slowly to a friend or silently to oneself.)

*S*it, *or lie down if necessary, in a position you find comfortable.*

Allow yourself to settle into this position so the whole body feels present. Take your time.

Begin to focus the attention on the discomfort, whether physical or mental. Just let it be there.

Begin to bring the awareness toward the feelings and sensations in the area of investigation. Not trying to change it. Just observing.

Any tension around that pain? A wanting to run?

Just let yourself feel whatever arises there.

Is there fear and resistance denying the heart access to this hurting mind/body?

Notice any feeling of opposition to fully opening to this discomfort. Opposition is resistance.

Is there a feeling of rising difficulty?

As the mind opposes the body, tightness?

The difficulty is the resistance to difficulty itself. What turns discomfort to pain ultimately turns pain to suffering. The wish to push it away, to control it, to make it otherwise.

Resistance arises uninvited. Once it is there, invite it in. Open to it. Investigate it.

Just settle back for a moment without resisting resistance. Without pushing away the aversion to pain. Allow resistance to come into a non-resisting space of awareness that embraces it without judgement or fear.

Where are the sensations of resistance to be found in the body?

Every mental state has an associated body imprint.

What is the body pattern of resistance?

Is there more sensation on one side of the body than the other?

Where is your tongue in your mouth? Pressed up against the palate? Curled down to the floor of the mouth? Pressed against the lower teeth?

Notice the tendency for the mind and body to try to close off discomfort, to ostracize it.

Picture that fist of resistance that closes around our pain.

Notice how that fist holds to the pain and won't let it go. Won't allow it simply to be. Notice how it turns the unpleasant into an emergency. Where is there room for our life?

See this white-knuckled clinging to our pain that distorts it into suffering.

Watch how the body holds, captures, each sensation.

Watch how the mind clenches against the unwanted.

And begin gradually to open around that closedness. The least resistance can be so painful. Open.

Soften.

Let the sensations and feelings float in a merciful awareness.

Let them be received as is, constantly changing moment-to-moment.

All around the sensations, the feelings, soften.

Allow the fist moment-to-moment to open. Picture the fingers surrendering one by one the pain. Giving space for the sensations and feelings to be experienced in mercy and awareness.

Allowing the dissatisfactory to be received openhandedly by a merciful awareness.

Let go of the pain. Why hold on a moment longer? Let it go. Let it be.

Let go of the holding that creates suffering.

Not pushing it away but letting it be in mercy and a soft receptivity.

Softening all around sensation, all around feelings, the fist of resistance loosening, opening, letting go at last. Letting be at last.

The palm of that fist softening. The fingers releasing their hold, opening. Opening all about sensation and feeling.

Moment-to-moment letting go, surrendering the fear that intensifies pain. Allowing sensations and feelings to arise naturally.

Tension dissolving in the softness.

The sensations, the feelings, dissipating at the edge. Moment-to-moment the sensations melting in the warm embrace of mercy and awareness.

Moment-to-moment letting go.

Moment-to-moment softening.

The fist open, the fingers having loosened their grip, sensation no longer imprisoned in resistance.

Opening. Floating free in the softness.

The pain softened at the edge, dissolving in space.

Resistance melted away.

Just moment-to-moment feeling, just moment-to-mo-

ment sensation, arising and dissolving in the soft spaciousness.

Resistance to pain, resistance to discomfort, resistance even to healing—that fist now opened to a deeper life.

Just receiving the moment in softness and care.

Awareness and sensation meeting, melting moment-to-moment.

The body, the mind, soft and open. Sensations and feelings arising and dissolving, floating free in the soft, open body. In the spacious mind.

Moment-to-moment letting go.

Moment-to-moment mercy and loving kindness.

Moment-to-moment releasing whatever holding remains. Even the subtlest twitch of resistance dissolving in the vastness.

Resistance to resistance dissolved in space.

Just this soft open spaciousness of being in which everything floats in a tender merciful awareness. A gentle letting go into the vast heart.

Letting go into the heart of being, into the mercy and loving kindness of your deep nature—beyond the body, beyond even the mind.

Vast edgeless space.

Just being.

In the spaciousness beyond the body, beyond the mind, the heart has room for it all.

Having explored the inner realms of afflictive resistance, it might be added here that resistance itself is not always unskillful (see Gandhi quote on p. 21). Resistance to injustice can be a matter of compassion. But still the fist needs to be opened to succeed. It is a matter for deep contemplation.

It seems odd that the idea of "nonresistance to evil" should be attributed to Jesus, who was a reformer. But when we recognize that all reformers (and those parts of ourself) are angry, the real question becomes how to resist the cruel without creating more of the same.

We cultivate just such a noninjurious resistance when we decide in ourselves to at last go no further on old, unskillful paths. For it is when the mind cries out that *nothing* is worth the heart being closed a moment longer that we pull ourselves free of long unsatisfactory patterns. This is the resistance which is a conscious response to unconscious reaction. It is another aspect of the path of light.

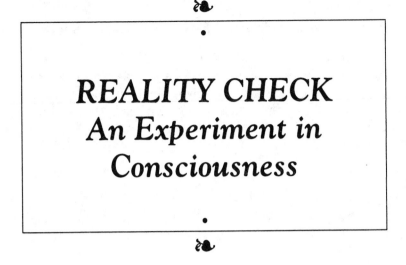

REALITY CHECK
An Experiment in Consciousness

To increase daily clarity we need be clear about what is happening while it is happening. Noting helps. But the mind is often swept away by desire or fear, lost in hard-bellied thoughts of control and helplessness.

To meet all of ourselves, some continuity is required. We cannot leave our meditation on the cushion and expect our daily lives to support a merciful wisdom. We may need to return a hundred times a day to soft belly. But first we need be aware that the belly is tight, that the mind is holding.

Just as noting supports recognition of what is happening while it is happening, this "reality check" encourages investigation midstream, in the midst of the momentum of our daily lives. It illuminates our drowsy blindness. It liberates the moment and deepens our sense of ease and play.

195

Practices that bring insight into our daily lives reflect the healing we seek. Such investigations as this allow us to keep abreast of ourselves, to stay in the heart of the matter.

It is part of the lightening which leads to enlightenment.

CHECK THE BODY—
belly tight?
How's your sphincter?
Grinders grasping?
What is the body pattern?
Where is the tongue in the mouth?
On the palate? Upper teeth? Lower teeth?
Curled down, pressed against the lower mandible?
Is there tension in the throat?
A hard swallowing away of some inner truth?
How's your heart?

CHECK THE MIND—
what is the state of mind?
Is it pleasant or unpleasant?
Is there a complaining?
What is the tone of the inner voice?
Is it speaking to you or at you?
Is there judgement?
Aggression?
Fear?
How does wishful thinking keep the pain fresh?
Resistance?
How does softening and letting go around these feelings affect this state?

CHECK THE HEART—
does the chest feel tight?

Is there sadness there?
Doubt?
Fear?
Anger?
Joy?
Is there grief?

Whatever is found in the body, in the mind, in the heart, open to it.

Breathe the breath of the heart into it.

Sense the peace beneath.

How does the rest of the body/mind respond to this gradually opening softness?

Does the breath connect through any armoring or resistance with the sacred heart beneath?

What does that "still small voice within" suggest?

ON WORKING
WITH PAIN

Pain moves like the breath
in the mind
to form the body.

Pain makes the body
so small
we forget our real body—
the body of being
from which this tiny
tight-bellied,
born
and dying flesh emerges.

Some say, "Pain is love"
they've panicked!—
but pain does remind us

again and again
how much mercy
is needed
to be whole
and how love heals
the deeply wounded
and reaffirms the earth
beneath our feet.

When pain is met by love
the world of suffering dissolves.

When pain is met
in the heart—
softening the body
and the mind—
the room expands,
the walls fall away
and we are left alone
with the mystery
of being
who we really are
even as the body weeps
but does not close
and the pain begins
to float
in something greater.

And in this opening
into the pain
nothing is added
or deferred—
just this
in the heart of mercy—
no suffering
anywhere.

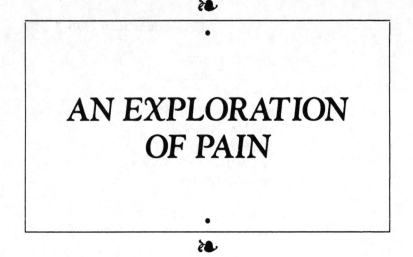

AN EXPLORATION
OF PAIN

The ability to work with pain comes gradually. To work with pain means to become accustomed to the resistance that automatically attempts to intercede. Acknowledging this unwillingness to go further we learn to soften, to give pain space, so that it might eventually be able to simply float in awareness rather than be rejected by it.

We are conditioned to react to our pain with fear and a sense of emergency. We walk across the floor and stub our toe. What kind of reaction mechanically arises? Do we send loving kindness and a soft spaciousness into that throbbing toe? Do we let the sensations spire out into space and dissolve, embracing them with mercy and loving kindness? Is there consciousness of the process by which we turn pain into suffering? Or do we ostracize the pain, send hatred into it, and then feel helpless by our inability to control it? Does resistance reinforce old boundaries which hinder healing?

We turn pain to suffering by attempting to escape. By not opening to the moment. By not allowing our amazing capacity for spaciousness to float lightly what seemed so heavy a moment before. To explore discomfort is called "entering the pain that ends suffering." It is the direct experience of the multiple sensations that constellate to form what we nervously label pain. It is a direct approach to these sensations before they fall into the deep ruts and long skidmarks of our resistant panic at discomfort.

To enter the pain that ends suffering is to enter discomfort with a merciful awareness. To respond from the spaciousness of the heart to the tightened mind/body. Noting changing states of mind. Remembering soft belly. Watching old reactive patterns retreat and melt into the process.

Pain stimulates grief. It uncovers deep, latent tendencies, feelings of isolation and aggression, of abandonment and distrust. It amplifies judgement, helplessness, and fear. And our resistance batters what we have come to call our "inner child" with guilt and a sense of failure and hopelessness.

Indeed, working with pain is not unlike opening to grief. Usually neither are approached with any mindfulness or care until the pain has become a suffering so great it overwhelms even our heart-resistant denial. But by then one can hardly get any space at all in which to settle back into the heart to view with merciful dispassion the fiery passions pain has stimulated.

If you and I walk into a gymnasium and first try to pick up a 300-pound weight, you and I, even together, may be unable to do so. We will become herniated—strained and muscle-fatigued, and doubting of our capacity to lift anything at all. But we can work with the 5- and 10-pound weights all day. And develop whatever our capacity allows.

As in working with grief and exploring with heart our

everyday ordinary grieving, one can not wait until the loss or pain is so great that its suffering obscures the sun. We learn to work with the great grief by opening to the smaller moments of loss and feelings of isolation. If one waits until pain is tormenting or one is in agony (a 300-pound weight), it will probably be very difficult to get any openness at all around the feelings of so little openness. So we learn to work with the lesser pains, the 10- and 20-pound weights, the minor abrasions and sore throats, to open a relationship between discomfort and the heart without becoming lost in the fearful escape modalities that labyrinth the mind.

Having cultivated little openness to lesser pains, we find ourselves atrophied in the wake of greater discomforts. So few unpleasantries investigated—ostracizing the stubbed toe, we retract the heart and leave only suffering.

Exploring lesser moments of discomfort we come to understand something of the nature of discomfort itself. And the frightened scrambling mind. We learn from the inside how resistance magnifies pain and how to let go. How to simply be when what is not wished for is nonetheless forthcoming. It is again a moment in which we learn that we will never know how to be happy until we have learned to relate heartfully to unhappiness. Or as a friend says, "You can't be happy 'til you learn how to be unhappy."

The grief that arises to meet our pain is the long submerged holdings, the residue of previous victories and defeats, that surfaces when the mind feels helpless, sees "no way out." These holdings come to reinforce the pain and broaden its dimension to suffering.

The longest chapter in *Who Dies?* is about working with pain. Rather than reiterate that lengthy investigation we refer you to that material.

The key word in working with physical (as well as mental) pain is "softening." It has the power to transmit the spaciousness required for a deeper investigation and letting go.

Because pain has a similar quality to grief, in that it can bring into awareness the submerged holdings of a lifetime, it also has the power of enormous purification, healing, and liberation. Materials that are often dug for on the psychiatrist's couch or yogi's cave for years, become instantly available to investigation. That which we were barely conscious of previously, what we refer to as "the unconscious," arises into consciousness. Knowing that we cannot let go of anything we do not accept, this accessibility of awareness to the previously buried, offers the possibility of a profound healing.

But it is easier said than done. It takes great mercy to work with pain. And sudden, intense pains may be too great to get much space around. But most are eventually available to the heart. It is our unwillingness to enter pain that often intensifies it. The uninvestigated 50-pound pain quickly becomes a 300-pound weight. Though we see how this process occurred and pledge yet deeper awareness, we may feel that it doesn't help much. We may be able to relate *to* our pain for only a few moments before the old conditioning to relate *from* that pain, from grief, reasserts itself. We may feel this is too inconsequential to matter. But in truth we are conditioning, in any moment of openness, openness to the next moment. We slowly clear the way. In any situation where movement is particularly difficult, the least movement becomes of great value. Great healing is available in tiny movements of awareness toward objects from which we have previously withdrawn. It is as Thomas Merton said, "True love and prayer are learned in the moment when prayer has become impossible and the heart has turned to stone."

When pain stimulates grief, the mind calls out for mercy and the heart offers the healing. The deeper the wound, the deeper the heart goes to embrace it. The closer to the surface wounds arise, the more directly they can be followed to their root by a merciful penetrating awareness.

So the opening to grief offers the end of grief, in the same way that entering pain can end suffering.

The harder we pull away, the tighter the noose becomes. To move toward the unwanted with a merciful awareness is to loosen our bonds. To enter directly that which has so often been rejected and reviled by our fear is to participate in the healing of a lifetime.

A GUIDED MEDITATION ON SOFTENING PAIN, PAIN I

(To be read slowly to a friend or silently to oneself.)

*T*ry to find a comfortable position and settle into it.

Slowly allow your attention to move toward the area of discomfort.

Watch what feelings arise as you let your awareness approach that place.

Let the pain just be there.

Is the mind and body at war? Much resistance? Is the mind cursing the body?

Is there any fear accumulated in the area of discomfort?

Notice if any old mind fears cling there, turning pain to suffering. Resistance to hellishness.

Notice whatever feelings arise in that area.

Begin to soften all about physical and mental discomfort.

Let the skin, the flesh, the muscles, begin to soften all around the pain.

Let the fist of resistance and fear which closes down around the unpleasant slowly begin to open. Releasing

205

tension around discomfort. Letting go of the rigidity holding unwanted sensations.

Let go. This holding, this old resistance and dread turns
the moment sour.

Let go. It is so painful to hold to the pain with anger
and fear and hopelessness. Let it go.

Let it begin to float in awareness instead of being
trapped hard in the body.

Moment to moment sensation arises. Moment to moment opening. Softening to each particle of sensation.

Let the muscles soften.

Let the flesh open to receive the moment as it is in
mercy and loving kindness. The fear, the anger, the sense
of failure dissolving into the softness.

Each moment new.

Softening from sensation to sensation.

Notice how the least thought or subtlest holding rees-
tablishes tension. Soften. Moment to moment letting go.

Remembering the mercy that pain cries out for—soften
again and again and once again.

Let the discomfort just be there, not holding to it, not
even pushing it away.

Softening to the very center of each instant of sensation
and feeling.

Meeting the heart of our pain in mercy and forgiveness.

Moving gently into it to heal, to release so much
frustration, so much helplessness. Allowing at last the
moment simply to be as it is with such mercy for ourselves
and these sensations arising in soft flesh.

Soften the ligaments.

Soften the tissue all around each sensation. Let each
sensation float free in this softness. Letting it be in the
heart of mercy and kindness toward oneself, toward this
moment, toward these sensations constantly changing.

Open all around sensation gently.

Push nothing away.

Let resistance melt from the body with a sigh. Let go of long-held fear and doubt.

And in the mind that holds to this pain, that prays to it and wars with it, that beseeches it, a deeper softening begins to permeate. The mental fist opens.

Feel the release of tension in the mind as it softens to the unpleasant in the body. Have mercy.

A moment of fear, a moment of distrust, a moment of anger—each arising and dissolving, one after the other. Each mind-moment dissolving into the next. The spaciousness increasing.

Hard reactions melting to soft responses in the mind. The body softening to receive the moment as is.

Moment-to-moment softening all about sensations arising.

Softening the tissue. Softening the muscles. Softening around each moment of experience arising in the body.

Softening to the center of each cell.

Sending mercy and loving kindness into each moment of sensation arising and dissolving in space.

Each instant of sensation received in an awareness that gently embraces.

Letting go of discomfort.

Letting it float in a merciful awareness.

Letting the mind float in the heart.

Receiving this moment in the opening heart of mercy.

Receiving this softness in all the far-flung galaxies of the body.

In the vast body, such mercy, such kindness, receives each moment.

Softening. Opening with a merciful awareness we continue the path of the healing we took birth for.

A GUIDED MEDITATION ON LETTING PAIN FLOAT, PAIN II

(To be read slowly to a friend or silently to oneself.)

*A*s the first meditation opens the body and becomes *your own, consider expanding the practice.*

Find a comfortable place to sit and when the body is soft and sensations are seen coming and going all by themselves, let the mind and body settle into that flow.

As you open to the body-moment, receive the mind in that same open spaciousness. Letting go all about sensations and feelings. Softening. Opening. The mind encouraged not to hold anywhere. Just observing the passing show, sensations arising and dissolving in soft tissue. Feelings and thoughts arising and dissolving in a spacious softness.

Letting go of thoughts. Just letting them run themselves out, watching them dissolve into their own natural impermanence. Floating in space for a moment. Vanishing into the process.

Let thought think itself in this spaciousness.

Whatever thought arises, let it float as it will. No interference.

Whatever sensation arises, let it float too in the vastness of being.

Thoughts, sensations, feelings, floating in this boundaryless spaciousness.

Not being the pain, not being even the thoughts about pain, just being itself, not leaning toward or away from anything.

Just an openness in which experience is unfolding as a moment of sensation, a moment of thought, a moment of feeling, a moment of smelling, of hearing, of tasting, of touching. Life unfolding moment to moment in a boundaryless spaciousness beyond definition.

A particle of fear arises, dissolving into a moment of doubt, dissolving into a new softening arising. Floating free.

Each mind-moment like a bubble floating in limitless space.

Sense the tininess of thought. Sense how thought dissolves moment to moment into process. Sense the vastness of awareness.

Sense the space in which this process floats.

Whatever arises in the mind or body is constantly changing. Doubt, confusion, expectation, fear, just let them all pass through. Don't hold anywhere.

Thoughts, like sensations, dissolve in space.

There one moment, vanished the next.

Confidence, relief, and trust arise from the heart that has room for even our discomfort. Old mind dissolving in this soft clarity.

Observe the ever-changing flow of these thoughts and sensations. Nothing stays for long, constantly arising, constantly disappearing into the flow of being.

Sensations float in the body, changing moment to moment.

The body softens to receive even the subtlest movement of sensation.

The mind softens too, receiving constant change as thought, as feeling, as sensation, as experience perpetually unfolding. The whole body soft, open, not holding, not pulling back, just allowing things to be as they are without the least interference.

Without the least clinging or condemning.

Sensations arising, thoughts arising, no resistance, no reaching out, no pushing away, no tightening, just soft open space.

Each moment experienced in softness.

Even the sound of my voice arising and dissolving in great spaciousness.

Hearing happening all by itself.

Nothing to do.

Just sound changing instant to instant within the vastness.

Feel this spaciousness of being which expands outward in every direction.

It encompasses each sound, each moment of thought, of sight, of feeling.

A moment of hearing followed by a moment of seeing, by a moment of thought.

All floating in the vast space of awareness, of beingness itself.

The sound of my voice.

A car passing in the street.

An airplane crossing overhead.

All occurring within the boundaryless spaciousness of awareness.

No boundary anywhere, awareness extends to the end of the universe and beyond.

Let the mind become like this great expanse of space.

Each experience like a cloud floating through this vastness.

Each feeling, each hearing, each seeing, each smelling constantly changing, folding in upon itself, dissolving in the vastness.

Sense how this awareness exists everywhere at once, extending out everywhere in all directions, boundaryless, receptive, universal.

The edgeless space of being no longer held to the outline of the body.

The whole field of sensation floating in edgeless space.

Awareness not limited to the small body, to these momentary sensations but extending outward everywhere, radiating into space.

Not contained even in the space of this room or in the atmosphere of this planet.

Awareness expanding into unlimited space.

Let this boundaryless awareness be the open mind which holds to nothing, which creates nothing, which impedes nothing. Which allows all things to pass without the least clinging or interference, observing sound, sight, memory, feeling, arising and dissolving each and every one in an enormous awareness.

Each sound arising and dissolving in the spaciousness.

Each sensation, each thought, each feeling floating in awareness.

No edges anywhere.

Limitless being unfolding in limitless awareness.

Body soft, sensations floating in vast space.

Mind open and clear, process unfolding in this endless spaciousness.

Let the edges of the body, of the mind, melt into the vastness.

Sensations, feelings, floating.

Each moment changing, floating free in pure awareness.

In this vast mind, the open heart, the body is received like a newborn into the arms of a loving mother.

Awareness embracing everything, holding to nothing, the mind dissolved in the vast heart.

Sensations floating free, dissolving in space.

Dissolving.

Just space.

Just peace.

AN EXPLORATION OF THE EMOTIONS AROUND PAIN

To soften the belly and explore pain in the mind/body may seem very unattractive. To open to levels of armoring around the heart, the grief, the anger, may even seem extreme. Cultivating mercy and awareness to receive discomfort in a new tenderness is an odd idea for many. For many to explore the breath inside the breath, the very beingness out of which life originates, may seem bizarre, even useless, in the face of their discomfort and confusion.

But for some, something in the heart is drawn toward using the difficult and the pained as a teaching that stimulates the possibility of deeper levels of healing and love.

We have seen many people start to direct a merciful awareness into their mental and physical wounds, their illnesses, and deeply affect the course of their cancer, their degenerative heart disease, their fears, their depression, their AIDS, their ALS, their multiple sclerosis. Although all did not experience their body as cured, many began to experience a deeper healing. For the first time a new satisfactoriness arose in that which had always seemed so dissatisfactory. Something within began to change its relationship to mental and physical pain. Even if the illness itself was not cured, the heart received a healing. For many the difficulties of the mind/body that originally drew them to investigate healing became less of a problem and more the focus of a new participation in life.

It is not difficult to recognize how merciless we are with ourselves and how deeply conditioned we are to escape. Returning to the image of the stubbed toe. Notice how we inundate our pain with disgust and aversion. We feel betrayed. We hate it. We push it away just when it most needs the heart's connection and the soft embrace of mercy. Just when an expansive letting go might allow the healing in, we close. But instead of *reacting* to the pain, imagine responding by allowing these sensations to be received and felt fully in a merciful awareness. Just letting the sensations be there, experiencing themselves, floating in compassion. Met by a softness and care that didn't create or hold to pain but simply accepted the moment as it is. Imagine how much it might affect our daily lives if we connected the heart with the disheartened!

One may enter almost any pain in the mind or body and discover around it some unfinished business in the shadow of our mercilessness. Have mercy on the tired mind. As awareness approaches pain, these sensations are rhythmically punctuated by the associated thoughts and feelings which automatically surround discomfort. Perhaps a bit of anger or shame or guilt encompass it. A vision of oneself as a failure or perhaps a sense of not enoughness. Because we have only learned to react to pain with fear we perhaps experience self-pity. The mind indicts the pain, and the pained as well. It says, "I deserve it" or "How stupid could

I be to let this happen to me?" We are so merciless with ourselves. We often find little room for ourselves in our hearts when we most require it. So much of our mental and physical pain is met with resistance and anger, so little of ourselves available to healing.

There is nothing to judge in the anger or fear or even judgement that surrounds our pain. Of course it's there at times! Big surprise! No blame. But uninvestigated and stuffed below the level of awareness, this pain/grief burns the heart and makes the moment unbearable. So much self-hatred gathers about the pain. So much to repel healing. But heartfully explored, the blockages to healing become the guideposts of the path to liberation.

A GUIDED MEDITATION ON THE EMOTIONS AROUND PAIN, PAIN III

(To be read slowly to a friend or silently to oneself.)

*L*et your eyes close and bring your attention to the breath.

Let awareness come to the level of sensation.

As awareness begins to establish itself in the moment, allow it to approach the area of discomfort.

Just feel what is there. Nothing to change. Nothing to do about it.

Just sensations arising in the moment.

Let it all be just as it is.

As awareness approaches the area of discomfort, is there any tension noticed, any rigidity that it must pass through?

Is there a pushing away of this investigation? An unwillingness to go further?

Just notice whatever resistance might arise.

Notice what limits the approach of awareness.

Is there a quality of holding around the area of discomfort?

Examine it. No need to change anything.

Receive the moment as it is.

Nothing to define. Just allowing a willingness to know, just allowing a not knowing, to receive the moment.

As awareness makes contact with the sensations that arise in the area of discomfort, what feelings are present in the moment-to-moment flow around sensation?

Does thought arise? Do certain feelings accompany unpleasant sensations? Do other images arise?

What are the voices around pain?

What is the tone of voice of the feelings that huddle around the unpleasant?

Do they repeat a certain theme? A certain state of mind?

What emotions are noticed there?

Is there fear or shame?

Is there anger or doubt?

Nothing to create, just receiving the moment as it presents itself in a receptive awareness.

Do any of these feelings limit the entrance of mercy into the pain?

Do any of these feelings seem to resist letting the healing in?

Is there unfinished business around the pain? Is there some grief? A sense of betrayal? Feelings of failure?

So little mercy we have for ourselves.

Is there a sense of urgency in the mind which creates a stiffness in the body, a holding around pain?

Has life become an emergency?

Are there feelings, moods, held in the body, associated with discomfort?

Is there guilt or doubt? Feelings of betrayal?

Is there a sense of helplessness or hopelessness?

Does this grief around pain free it or enslave it?

Have mercy on yourself. Soften to the holding.
Soften the discomfort.

Allow the body to open and soften around whatever hindrances, whatever holdings present themselves.

Soften the tissue all around discomfort—let it begin to float in a merciful awareness.

Let the body cradle its hurt places as if it were embracing its only child.

Nothing to push away.

Opening moment to moment all around sensation. Softening the tissue, the flesh, the hardness around sensation.

Allowing sensation to be received in a merciful softness, a willingness to meet it with kindness rather than grasping it in fear and trembling. A willingness to let it go, to let it float in the vast space of the heart.

Whatever attitudes, feelings, or thoughts accompany discomfort, let them float too.

Let the whole mind and body be received moment to moment in mercy and softness.

Whatever arises into awareness, just let it be.

Notice how judgement or fear or even a longing for healing can tighten the area.

Let these mental images come and go. Notice how even expectation can create tension and let it too float in the vast spaciousness of awareness.

Watch how a hard thought can harden the body. See this process soften to it. Notice how feelings can amplify discomfort.

And soften yet more deeply.

Observe how softening lets it all float in edgeless awareness.

Allow each sensation and each moment of feeling to arise and dissolve in soft, open space.

Receive each particle of emotion or sensation as if for the very first time.

Acknowledging even the slightest tension or holding in a soft, allowing awareness, let the healing in.

Just allow the open space of a merciful awareness to receive the constant flow of change in the area of discomfort.

Receiving constantly changing feelings, sensations, moods, hopes, fears, and the deeper healings which present themselves when we hold nowhere.

Let all that arises in the mind body come and go with mercy and awareness.

Let the heart receive it all. Healing entering directly, finishing business. Letting go of the suffering so the pain can float in a loving kindness the aching body longs for.

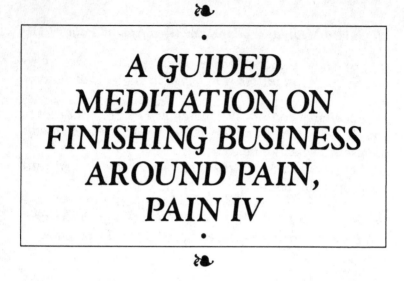

A GUIDED
MEDITATION ON
FINISHING BUSINESS
AROUND PAIN,
PAIN IV

(To be read slowly to a friend or silently to oneself.)

[This is a variation on the exploration of Emotions Around Pain meditation. It may be particularly useful to those working with serious illnesses of questionable prognosis.]

Find a comfortable place to sit and let your eyes close.
Bring your attention to the breath.
Let awareness focus on the sensations that accompany each breath.
Gradually allow awareness to come to the level of sensation.
Feel the breath as it passes in and out of the nostrils.
Focus on the moment-to-moment sensation that accompanies each inhalation and each exhalation.
Mindfulness of breathing.

As awareness settles into the level of sensation, besides the breath, other sensations are felt in the body.

Allow the attention to move toward these other sensations.

Does the mind label these pain? Just notice what is happening.

Nothing to create.

Just the moment as it is in clear awareness.

Allow awareness to approach more closely these sensations.

Let awareness approach the center of the moment-to-moment sensations arising in that area.

As awareness attempts to approach the moment-to-moment sensations in that area, what is felt?

What emotions cluster around these sensations?

Various states of mind arise to "protect the pain." But turn it to suffering.

Is some stress noticed around these sensations? A sense of betrayal?

Is there fear resisting the entrance of awareness?

Is there anger or shame around the pain?

How does anger differ from shame?

And where is love and forgiveness?

Explore in the silence whatever feelings arise around discomfiture.

Are these feelings a kind of unfinished business with the unpleasant in our lives? A kind of grief? Are they the lamentations of those parts of ourselves we have still not integrated into our heart?

Nothing to judge, but note judgement if it arises.

Does judgement accompany pain?

Nothing to fear, but note fearfulness if it is present.

Does fear accompany the unpleasant?

No reason to doubt your ability to heal, but note doubt if it encapsulates the pain.

Does doubt limit further progress?

Cure comes or does not come to the body. But healing is a matter of the heart.

Let the belly soften to receive the moment in mercy.

There is a healing we took birth for. Each moment is it.

To open the heart in hell, to make peace where once there was war.

Even if the body goes its own way the heart will know that way and beyond.

Forgiveness settles unfinished business.

Turning toward that unfinished mental pain that surrounds physical discomfort begin to send mercy into the center of the moment-to-moment sensations that arise in that area.

Forgive this poor body. Have mercy on you.

And forgive the fear and anger and shame that constellate uninvited around pain.

Just note their natural presence with a soft awareness. Send forgiveness to the pains of the mind and body that they may be received by the heart rather than leaving us lost in the mind.

There is grace when the heart touches the disheartened.

Turn to your body, as if it were your only child, and say, "I forgive you."

Let awareness enter the moment-to-moment sensation arising and dissolving in the vast spaciousness of being.

Allow a merciful awareness to receive gently the feelings and sensations in the area of discomfort.

Not attempting to change anything. Force closes the heart. Just receiving in mercy and loving kindness this body of sensation, this mind of feelings, of fears and doubts, of bewilderment and hope.

Have mercy on you. Let the sensations, let the feelings float in the vast spaciousness of awareness, not holding to anything, not pushing anything away.

Just mercy and awareness meeting feeling and sensation

moment-to-moment as they arise and dissolve in the flow of consciousness.

Let the heart receive the body and the mind with a healing kindness and care that softens to each sensation. Let it all come and let it all go in mercy and awareness.

KARMA SAVINGS
AND LOAN

At Karma Savings and Loan your principal accrues from your interests. Karma is based on intention. It is a beneficent process which keeps reminding us to let go and be merciful. It sends out regular statements that the wisdom of the heart is the coin of the realm.

Don't become overdrawn at Karma Savings and Loan. Pay attention. And if indeed you are temporarily overdue on a payment, don't write a bad check—open the heart, respond with mercy and awareness. Though each is born with an active account, karma need not be just more unfinished business, a constant checking of the balance sheet. To go beyond your karma, beyond reaction to response, give up your account, give it all to the sacred. Follow your heart. Trust the process.

AN EXPLORATION INTO HEALING

Balance arises when we enter with mercy and awareness areas that have been withdrawn from in fear and anger. Healing is a rehabitation of deserted areas of the mind/body. A living of our whole life.

When that merciful clarity receives the long-abandoned, and accepts the ever-rejected, there is a moment of silence. The voice of our suffering does not attempt to reestablish domain. Old mind can no longer maintain its accustomed imbalance. The muttered contents of the mind dissolve into the process of the heart. And the heart bursts into flame and opens to the healing we took birth for.

Investigation heals, because wherever awareness is focused, a natural balance eventually resumes. Healing follows awareness. Healing in the mind or the body follows the same path. First we acknowledge the pain. And soften to hard places. Soft-belly meditation. We change direction from withdrawal to approach. It is a "reversal of fortune." Resistance dissolves into a willingness to heal as we continue exploring the attitudes encountered approaching the discomfited. Healing the "unhealed."

Meeting the long-rejected with a new mercy, with a deepening awareness. Investigating the relationship between the feeling mind and the felt body. Opening to the unexplored.

This healing process continues as a direct entrance of awareness into the sensations in the area calling for healing. A brailling from moment to moment of the texture and changing forms we call sensation or pain. Exploring microscopically the moment-to-moment flow of consciousness in the body. Knowing the area "by heart."

Investigating the nature of pain and the vastness in which it floats we develop a familiarity with these sensations which become a conduit between the heart and the disheartened. Sensations attracting loving kindness.

Letting go of our suffering, we let the healing in. Trusting the process. Opening to the immensity, allowing in the healing which goes beyond even cure. That which our deep homesickness has navigated toward our whole lives when we were still enough to hear the heart.

And the area of pain becomes a focal point for mercy and awareness. The area once tensed to the unpleasant opens to the kindness flooding the area. Hard sensations softening at the edge. Dissolving in something even greater than our fear. Dissolving in the heart of the matter. Each sensation received as if it were our only child. Embraced tenderly by a merciful awareness that seeks only its liberation.

Healing is the process of a lifetime. Indeed, Ondrea and I have written *Healing into Life and Death* to explore this subject. As it says, healing is an open book and the secret to healing is that there is no secret at all. Healing uncovers the heart.

A GUIDED HEALING
MEDITATION

(To be read slowly to a friend or silently to oneself.)

Come to a sitting position if possible, or find a posture the body is able to maintain for a period of time. And feel the body that rests here.

Allow the attention to come into the body.

Feel the breath as it breathes itself in soft belly.

Let the body be soft and open.

Let the awareness be gentle and allowing.

Notice any area of the body that is in discomfort. Attending to the body, notice whatever sensation distinctly draws the attention.

Gently allow awareness to move toward the place that wants healing.

In this gentle approach toward discomfort soften to any resistance, any tension or restlessness which wanting or fearing may have created in the body. Observe how even denial or guilt can create an unwillingness to go further.

Slowly, without the least force, allow awareness to approach the sensations generated in this area.

227

And begin to soften all around the sensations.
Letting the flesh soften to allow awareness in.
Softening.
Let space begin to open all about this area.
Gradually opening.
Softening all about sensation.
Softening the muscles.
Softening the tissue in which sensation arises.
Softening the tendons, softening the flesh.
Softening even the bone.

Flesh gently opening, body softening to a merciful awareness.

Allowing sensation to be as it is in soft tissue.

Feel the fibers in the muscles releasing their grasp, softening. Letting go of pain.

Tendons softening. Flesh softening. Skin softening.

Allowing sensation to float in soft flesh.
Softening.
Letting go all about sensation.
In soft body, in soft mind, just letting it be there.

Meeting the moment-to-moment sensations with a moment-to-moment softening.

Softening the bone.
Softening to the very marrow.

Any tension that momentarily asserts itself allowed to float free.

Let it come. Let it go.
Moment-to-moment sensation arising in soft awareness.

Gently, without force, gradually opening the tissue to let sensation float.

Softening to the very center of the cells.
Awareness receiving sensation in soft open space.
Sensations floating in awareness.

The skin, the tissue, the muscles, the tendons soft and pliant. Spacious.

Flesh soft, allowing, willing.

Awareness receiving moment-to-moment sensation in a merciful softness.

Moment-to-moment sensation arising, floating in awareness, dissolving in the flow.

Awareness opening to even the subtlest flutter, the subtlest motion of sensation.

Softly.

Clearly.

Softening the body all about discomfort, let awareness approach directly these sensations with the explorer's eye.

Awareness investigating sensation floating in space.

Do the sensations stay still or do they move?

Do sensations have an edge?

Does the area of sensation have a shape?

Does that shape stay constant or is it constantly changing?

Moment-to-moment sensation floating in a soft, merciful awareness that simply explores the moment.

Do these sensations have density? Are they thin or thick?

Are they round? Are they flat?

Moment-to-moment sensation received in moment-to-moment awareness.

Discovering the nature of sensation.

Do these sensations have a texture?

Are they rough? Are they smooth?

Do they stay the same? Do they vary?

Sensations floating in space.

Soft flesh, muscles eased and opened, tissue allowing and merciful.

Notice whatever thoughts or feelings accompany the mind's deeply conditioned reaction to what it labels "pain."

Are there feelings that harden the area? Doubt or fear? Helplessness or hopelessness?

Investigating the moment as feeling.

Does the area of sensation complain of being isolated? Is it shunned by the body?

Levels and levels of softening all about sensation.

Explore the moment as it is.

Like sensation, let thoughts and feelings too float in the vast spaciousness of awareness.

A merciful awareness receiving sensations and their attendant feelings moment to moment.

Opening to even the least tension in the mind that closes the body. Soften all about it.

A deeper letting go. A deeper letting be. Softening.

Are there tendrils that connect this area with other areas of sensation in the body?

Moment-to-moment awareness.

Moment-to-moment sensation.

Moment-to-moment softening, allowing, receiving.

Investigating sensation arising and dissolving in vast space.

Are the sensations soft or hard?

Are they hot or cold? Or neither?

Is there a feeling of pressure? A vibratoriness? A movement?

Soft awareness opening into a vast spaciousness which allows sensation to unfold moment to moment in the clear light of a merciful awareness.

Exploring sensation as it arises instant to instant.

Nothing to create, just receiving what is.

Is there a sound there? Do these sensations have a voice? A tone of voice?

Is the voice familiar? What does it have to say?

Noticing softly, caringly, what these sensations which have been gagged by denial and resistance, by fear and loathing for so long, have to say.

Listen with the heart, to the pained mind, in the pained body.

Meet them with a soft, allowing awareness.

Have mercy on these orphaned voices. Listen. And listen again.

Sensations arising and dissolving in a merciful awareness.

Relating to this area, to these sensations as if they were your only child, meet them with love, with kindness and mercy.

Sensations floating in a soft, open awareness met with caring and mercy.

Does some image arise there? Is there color there? Just noting whatever is there, nothing to create.

Just receiving sensation in loving kindness and care.

Touching it all with mercy. Meeting it with forgiveness.

Each sensation received in the warmth and patience that is forgiveness.

Each sensation absorbed in loving kindness and mercy.

Allowing mercy to absorb each sensation.

Allowing sensation to float in the softness, in the spacious heart of being.

Floating in compassion.

Floating in mercy.

Let the spacious heart absorb sensation moment to moment.

Let this area become the heart we all share.

Let the mercy you feel for the suffering in the world touch your pain as well.

Each moment of sensation received so gently. Moment-to-moment sensation arising and dissolving in a vast spaciousness.

Each sensation dissolving in compassion for all those in pain.

Each moment dissolving, dissolving in mercy and loving kindness.

Each moment melting into infinite compassion and kindness.

Sharing this healing with all sentient beings.

Melting the discomforts of the world in tender mercy.

Meeting these sensations with kindness, forgiveness, and compassion. Meeting the world we all share in a healing awareness.

Each moment floating.

Sending mercy and loving kindness into the body we all share.

Each particle of sensation floating in infinite compassion and care.

Each moment dissolving into the heart of healing.

Sensation floating like tiny sparks in a velvet darkness. Shimmering and dissolving in vast space.

Dissolving into this healing shared for the benefit of all beings everywhere.

May all beings be free from suffering.

May all beings be healed into the heart.

A WAKE-UP CALL
An Experiment in Conscious Living

·

D o you wake up on the in-breath or the out-breath? How soon after you wake up do you awaken?

It is a practice that Ondrea and I have been playing with for years. To notice immediately upon awakening, sometimes even before the eyelids have opened, that awakening is occurring.

To play with the practice of noting whether you wake up on the in-breath or the out-breath is a skillful way to start the day. And if it is not until noon that you recall the practice, does that thought arise on the in-breath or the out-breath?

In the course of intense practice one becomes so familiar with the breath that even if one should wake in the middle of the night there is an immediate recognition of the breath breathing itself. Profound awakenings and insights have occurred for many in the hours before dawn.

When awareness reenters the waking world and instantly alights on the breath, it stays for a moment in that spaciousness of being before "being this" and "being that" reasserts itself. Before we wake into the sleepless dream of our everyday ordinary grief.

And soon we awaken when we awake.

ON WORKING
WITH GRIEF

Along the path of healing that leads into the heart, one is called upon to examine grief. Grief is the binding alloy of the armoring about the heart. Like a fire touched, the mind recoils at losing what it holds most dear. As the mind contracts about its grief, the spaciousness of the heart often seems very distant.

Some believe they have no grief. This is another aspect of our rigid denial and self-protection. Some indeed may say, "I haven't lost anyone—why should I be grieving?" If only it were that simple.

Most think of grief as a momentous sadness, but it is much subtler than that. Everyone has grief. Everyone seems to have some unbalanced tally sheet with life, some unfinished business. An incompleteness with the past and with ourselves, a fatiguing self-consciousness, the predominant theme of the unfinished symphony of mind's yearning.

Our grief manifests as a self-judgement, as fear, as guilt, as anger and blame. It is that insistent mercilessness with ourselves and a world that we hardly let within. Our grief is our fear of loss, our fear of the unknown, our fear of death. Our fear of what is coming around the next unknown corner. Grief is the rope burns left behind when what we have held to most dearly is pulled out of reach, beyond our grasp.

At subtler levels one sees that the tendency of the mind to hold, to cling and condemn, to judge, is a daily aspect of our grief. A feeling of "not-enoughness" that longs to become otherwise.

As we begin to direct the energy of forgiveness to ourselves and others, voices may arise that try to block the way to giving and receiving. These voices tell us that we are unworthy and useless. It is where we feel separate from ourselves, so many parts of mind pushed away, so little heart allowed to express itself. We wonder, looking into the warped mirror of our self-image, why what is reflected back seems so distorted, so unacceptable, so unwhole, and unlovable. This is our common grief.

But even grief is workable. Opening the heart to the mind's pain, we find space to explore mercifully. Gently approaching the long-accumulated density of our grief, so long resisted with aversion and disgust, we discover the unexplored territory between the heart and mind. And we acknowledge, with the sigh of letting go, how often we have distrusted what we feel. Examining what we feel, not analyzing why, we discover the labyrinthine patterns of our grief and unfinished business, the skeletons of so many moments of life which became lost by the wayside. And the darkness of a thousand moments of helplessness and hopelessness is illuminated in a clear and merciful awareness. That which has seemed so untouchable in the past is cradled in the arms of forgiveness and compassion. The armoring begins to melt. The path to the heart becomes straight and clear, recognizing how this exploration of our common grief, of the ways of our old suffering, opens the path to joy. Those who know their pain and their grief most intimately seem to be the lightest and most healed of the beings we have met.

Some may be led to this meditation because they sense some unfinished business with a loved one's death. Others, drawn by the pain of illness in their body or the body of a loved one, wish to heal more deeply. Some come as supplicants to offer up the common grief of unfulfilled dreams and the multiple losses of an ever-changing world. Laying down the unnamed, unlabeled grief they are wearied from carrying.

This meditation connects with the tears unshed, the laughs unlaughed, the moments unlived. One need not have experienced the death of a loved one in order to find this exploration a useful endeavor. It makes room in our heart for our pain, for our healing, for our life.

CONVERTING THE GRIEFPOINT TO THE TOUCHPOINT OF THE HEART

At the center of the chest, on the sternum, the breast-bone, generally between the nipples, is the heart center. It is an energy focal point of considerable tenderness at times, particularly when strong feelings of grief, self-protectiveness, of fear or loss are present. This ache at the center of the chest is the griefpoint. It is a mind/body convergence point where long-accumulated mental pain (grief) has solidified in the body, thick as armoring. It is the long-held aloneness and fear, doubt and anger, so often swallowed down and stuffed into the opening to the heart. Another stone rolled into the mouth of the cave against our resurrection. This tender heart area, analogous to Conception 17 in the energy technology of acupuncture, is the griefpoint as well as the touchpoint of the heart. This conversion occurs as grief begins to sink from the mind of separation and fear, resistance and dread, into the heart of mercy and loving kindness and pure awareness. In the integration of our pain into our heart, there is no separation to be found, just a unity of being shared in all our lives.

A GUIDED GRIEF
MEDITATION

(To be read slowly to a friend or silently to oneself.)

*F*ind a comfortable place to sit in a quiet room.

Take a few moments to settle into the quietness.

Gradually bring your attention to the center of the chest.

Let awareness gather at that place of high sensitivity. Notice any ache at the center. Is there a physically painful quality to your mental longing?

With the thumb, press gently into this point of grief and love.

Begin gradually to exert pressure on that point. Feel the sternum, the bone beneath, as though it were the armoring over the opening to the heart. As though it were that which blocked entrance so often to your spacious nature.

Slowly, without force, but with mercy and steadiness, push into that point.

Press in gently but firmly. Let the pain into your heart. Breathe that pain through that point into your heart.

240

Stop pushing it away. Push into it instead.
Let it in.
Breathe that pain in through the griefpoint.
Let your thumb push steadily, but without force, into that ache, awareness entering deeply that point of sensation at the center of the chest. A merciful awareness, using the pressure on the griefpoint to enter through years of accumulated sediment of unfelt, unexpressed, unexamined feelings. Penetrating the exhaustion of our everyday, ordinary grief compressed hard as rock.

Push into the pain. Past the resistance to life. Past the fear, the self-doubt, the distrust.

Past feelings of being unsafe. Past all that holding around being unloved. Past the ten thousand moments of putting yourself out of your heart. The judgement, the longing, the anger.

Past years of hidden grief. The shame and secret fears, and unrequited loves we have spoken of to no one.

Let the pain in at last.
Have mercy on yourself.
Let it in.
Let life in at last. Breathe that pain into your heart. Past the holdings and armorings of a lifetime. Let it in. Let it in at last.

Let your heart break. All the losses, all the injuries, all the grief, of a lifetime dumped there, layer after layer holding you back from your life. Holding you out of your heart.

Push in. Breathe that into your heart.
Let your heart at last experience all those parts of your life you have pushed away.

So little room in our hearts for our pain. Let it in. Receive it with mercy instead of fear or judgement.

Cradle your pain in your heart. Let each breath gently rock that cradle.

All the pain in our heart we have tried so long not to

feel, now drawn in with each breath. All the headlines we try to push away. All the news of a suffering world. The whole world on fire within and without. So much grasping to the burning embers of our longing and our dread.

All those children starving with bulging bellies and watery eyes. The ten thousand flies that come to eat them.

All the women, all the men, who have been abused and are being abused at this very moment. All the suffering of the world unfolding in this very instant.

All of their pain. All of our pain.

Breathe it in. Let it in.

And your children will die.

And your grandchildren.

Breathe it in.

Fear says stop, but gently continue in mercy for yourself and the deep healing.

Push in gently to the fear. Gently but firmly. Not as punishment but as a willingness to go beyond old protections and devices for escape. Past the old fears. Have mercy on you. Let this pain you have been trying to elude come into the heart of healing.

So much pain.

So much posturing.

So much hiding there.

A lifetime of fear, of anger, of distrust.

Let it in. Let it in.

It is so hard to live with our hearts closed. It is so hard to live armored and frightened. Unavailable to life, to ourselves.

Have mercy.

Let the tender heart receive all those parts of you that say it is self-indulgent to forgive yourself. That cruel, merciless judgemental mind. That cold indifference toward the suffering of others and ourselves. Let these griefs dissolve into the opening heart.

Breathe them into your heart. Let them melt. Let them be healed.

Let us get on with our lives.

All the pain in this world, all the fear of this world. All the moments we have hated ourselves. All the moments we would have rather been dead, armored right there at the center of the chest, melting.

All the times we couldn't say what we wanted to because we were afraid we wouldn't be loved. All the times we wondered what love really was. All the times we were disappointed, there at the center of the chest.

So much holding. Breathe that pain into your heart. Let it in.

Let it in.

Each breath drawn in through the griefpoint carries the pain right into the center of our heart.

So much room in our heart for our pain when we let go of the armoring and resistance. It is difficult to open to this grief-pain in our tiny body, in our fragile mind, so breathe it into the enormous heart.

This heart of mercy drinks from our pain. Let it in.

All the fear that we are less than good in God's eyes, that we are not the beloved. Breathe it in.

All the fears that we have fallen out of grace, that we are cursed and unlovable held right there in the griefpoint. Breathe it in.

Breathe it in.

A lifetime of pain. Breathe it in.

Push into that point. Notice how part of our grief comes from trying to keep grief under control. This merci-lessness with which we reject ourselves repeatedly. This often unkind mind, this fearful child we carry.

Have mercy on you. Let it into your heart. Let it break your heart at last.

Let it in.

Our parents die.

Our lovers die.

Our children die.

All that we know is in constant change. Constantly being born and proceeding toward death.

The people we love most will at times suffer. There is nothing we can do to keep them from their pain. This world is so hard at times.

Breathe it in. Let it in.

And sometimes our loved ones kill themselves. They can't stand the pain, they can't get through the armoring to the healing just beneath. But you can get through it. Push into that point. That griefpoint in the heart center. Let it in. How long can you elude your life?

So much of ourselves pushed aside. So much shame and mercilessness. All the places we will not forgive ourselves. All the places we are diminished. The despair, the help-lessness, breathe it in.

Breathe it in.

Let the breath take the pain to the center of your heart.

The heart has room for it all. Let it in.

Have mercy on you. Let the pain in past the fear.

All the moments that we weren't loved and weren't loving.

All the parts of ourselves we've coldly disregarded, regarded with mercy at the griefpoint, warmly drawn into the healing heart. All the self-cruelty. All our unwilling-ness to love ourselves. All our judgement.

Each breath bringing old mind into the heart, melting in the embrace of such kindness and care.

Fear melting.

Doubt melting.

The armoring falling away, exposing the luminescent whorl of the heart center. Our shimmering nature discov-ered just beyond our pain. The sense of loss flickering in the enormity.

Each breath drawing in gratitude for the moments

shared with those we have loved and lost. And gratitude for the mystery of connection.

The fear of a lifetime melting into the heart. Push ever so gently into it. Breathe that healing mercy right into your heart. An enormous energy. Let it in.

Just let that energy into your heart.

Draw the shadows into the light.

The armor disintegrating.

The griefpoint dissolving into the touchpoint of the heart. Hard-edge sensations softening. Dissolving into loving kindness.

Bringing home the lost child. The heart embracing the mind with the soft breath of mercy and the tender caress of forgiveness.

As the griefpoint becomes the heartpoint, the body begins to hum. Feel the cells like a dry sponge absorbing this mercy and deep kindness.

As the griefpoint surrenders its pain to the heart the pained contents of the mind float in the spaciousness of mercy and awareness. The feelings of separation increasingly becoming a sense of inseparability from that loved one, from ourselves.

Now let your hand come gently away from the griefpoint, let your hands settle into your lap.

Take the pressure off that point.

And notice that there seems to be an opening where the ache used to be.

You can feel the touchpoint of the heart when you take your hand away.

Breathe in and out of that point. This is the breath of the heart. Let awareness of the flow between the world and your heart be your constant companion.

Let the pain which drew your attention to the heart be an initiation into the healing you took birth for.

May all beings be free of suffering.

May all beings focus the spacious heart on the pained mind.

May all beings know the joy of their great deathless nature.

AN EXPLORATION
OF GRIEF

The application of the grief meditation, the intense work of opening our heart in hell, can be most useful. By finding the touchpoint of grief, one discovers the touch-point of the heart. Once again, our greatest suffering leads us toward the possibility of our greatest liberation. There is not somewhere else to go. One is constantly arriving. All the work is done in "just this much."

All of us have grief to explore, the grief of incomple-tion, of not having what we wish, the loss of face or actually the loss of facade, the despair of no control in the shifting sands of impermanence, in the ever-varying winds of an unknown universe. It is the death of friends. It is the loss of one's pet as a child. It is good friends moving away and old pains returning. It is all the moments of being unloved. It is the millions abused by those in power. It is that half of the world goes to sleep hungry. It is the impermanent body. It is the loss of faith. It is all the world-weariness, the fatigue of the struggle, the loss of love, the carelessness of certain actions that congeal around the heart. It is the ordinary grief, our unfinished business, our daily dying out of life. It is all that remains unlived in the preciousness of "just this much."

Often, however, it takes the loss of a loved one for us to notice the grief that has always been there. But even in the intense grief experienced in the death of a loved one, we recognize that nothing in grief is new. Grief is just old mind never before so intensely experienced. The ancient guardians of our self-image, the blockages of the heart, become uniquely evident. The fear, the self-judgement, the heaviness of body dense with doubt, the guilt and anger of so many lost moments, feelings of failure, trepidation, loathing, dread, and helplessness arise from just beneath the surface to present themselves in a blaze of anguished emotions. None of these qualities or experiences are new, though few have appeared with such intensity before. Little of our ordinary grief has been acknowledged.

In intense grief of loss we rediscover, unmistakably this time, the grief we have always carried, the ordinary grief that inhabits and inhibits our life. Some call this ordinary grief "angst." Many experience it as discomforting self-consciousness. Some experience it as jealousy, others as nationalism. But always it is accompanied by a deep sense of isolation and separation. It is the daily narrowing of perception that allows so little in. It is the envy and judgement of a lifetime, that everyday sense of loss. It is our homesickness.

Many people we talk with tend to equate death with God. Death is not God. Coming home is not something we can only do later, but something available to us right now, in each moment we are open to. To the degree we appreciate the light now, we still stay with the light then. Death is not God, any more than a magic trick is the magician. And just as a magician might show you after performing a trick how it was done, so too perhaps after death we might gain insight into the trick itself. As the death trick loses its mysteriousness, it tunes us deeper to an edgeless entry into the mystery itself. God is not someone or something separate, but is the suchness in each moment, the underlying reality. Like birth, or illness, or old age, death is just another event along the way. In fact, like birth, illness, and old age, death has a universal quality—it is nothing special. It is as common as God, inherent in every moment.

Do not mistake death for the divine. Do not be looking elsewhere for your true nature. Do not think of it as something coming, but instead recognize it as the ever-present possibility in each moment. If we do not examine the grief of our homesickness for God now, we will always be looking elsewhere for our healing. Death is not going home. Our home is the heart, our real nature. God is "just this much," the vast spaciousness of our inherent nature, luminous and whole, the heart of the moment.

Grief takes many guises. It is not a single state of mind but a generic label for a very specific process. During a retreat, after a particularly intense morning of investigating grief, a number of people came up to share their experiences. The first fellow who approached seemed quite agitated and said, "I am not grieving, I am not sad about the death of my father. I am angry as hell." The next woman who came up said, "I am not feeling grief, I am feeling anxiety." The next person said, "Well, I don't know if it's grief, but I feel kind of lost." The woman who approached next said, "What I am feeling isn't grief, it's guilt." Another spoke of shame, and the person following shared the deep self-doubts that had arisen after the suicide of her brother. Each felt they weren't "grieving correctly," but for each this was their process. These different states were the armoring that grief puts us in touch with. Each person was expressing the quality of the mind which had always blocked their deeper entrance within. For most, grief is more a word used to describe a feeling of being over-whelmed by loss than it is a definition of the multiple moods which constitute this most natural process. All of their feelings, all of their states of mind, were aspects of grief. There is no doing it right; there is just being with what is as wholeheartedly as the moment allows.

We expect our grief to be something special. In fact, our grief is as old as our self-image, so familiar that we often do not recognize it when it affects us. It has been there all our lives, but it is only with the impact of unmistakable loss that we acknowledge it. Perhaps if we recognized our ordinary grief sooner, we wouldn't be so overwhelmed by all that we have denied for so long. Opening to the little grief, the little losses, the little deaths, we make room for the greater griefs, the greater losses, the greater death. By making room in our heart for the lesser holdings, we cultivate the strength and presence for the greater.

Of the thousands we have worked with who were in the midst of deep grief, not a single person has said that the experience was altogether new. It was the same sadness, only deeper. It was the same anger, the same frustration, the same anxiety. The only thing that seemed to be new was that these feelings so powerfully arisen into conscious-ness could no longer be denied.

We have somehow wrestled our common everyday grief into submission, which is actually a submersion. We have learned to cope. This means, "I won't feel too much as long as I don't hurt too bad." It is quite a trade-off, and we grieve it.

But when some loss arises that we simply cannot deny, when it is our parents who have died, our husband, our wife, our lover, when it is our children's death, our best friend's, when it is our own body going through sickness and decay, then the ache we have carried for so long can no longer be ignored. Then the pain of a lifetime can no longer be suppressed. Feelings of separation or doubt or fear that have often caused us to withdraw from life and hide in safe territory are experienced in all their painful reality.

Grief is a process. It is not a single emotion, any more than anger or fear or doubt is. These are just sloppy labels we use to dull and remove ourselves from the intensity of so much work that is left unfinished, so much pain and fear and remorse gone uninvestigated. Someone asked, "Do I have to get rid of my anger before I can get into my grief?" Anger is our grief, and until it is acknowledged and investigated, it may be difficult to get into the feelings that lie beyond. For some it may be that until they explore whatever anger is felt toward the individual who died, they will not be able to experience the deeper healings that accompany a merciful awareness entering the subtler levels of their grief. Unexplored anger may separate them from the deeper levels of their grief in the same manner it has always separated them from the deeper levels of that person who is now grieved.

Actually that feeling of not grieving correctly, of being separate from grief, is grief itself. It is that feeling of separation from ourselves and others to which the word "grief" can most accurately be applied.

In our inquiry into the nature of mind, we quickly recognize just how much of a sense of separation resides there. It is in those feelings of isolation which the imagined self incorporates with such statements as "I am *this body*; I am *this mind*," that our ordinary grief is most evident. Within our grief, our pain, lies the unexamined, unarticulated craving for wholeness.

When we begin to acknowledge our everyday sense of isolation from that which we love most and with which we wish so dearly to merge, we begin to let go of the grief and pain that often encrust the heart.

When some people say they can't get into their grief, perhaps what they are saying is that they can't open to their anger, their fear, their doubt. They have put so many parts of themselves out of their heart, they have been coping with the mind so long, that now, with the death of a loved one, they are overwhelmed by the intensity of such feelings and find very little space in which to explore, to experience, to allow the history of their grief to manifest.

The acknowledgment of this long-held suffering is the first stage of healing into grief. We can no longer deny the reality of the long-submerged and, as in any healing, the first step is acceptance. We cannot let go of anything we do not accept. Investigation deepens our letting go. The fear which has always guarded these heavy emotions from exploration now becomes an object of examination and acts as a guide into new territory. Fear becomes an ally which whispers that we are coming to our edge, to un-plumbed depths, to the space in which all growth occurs. We discover that we have never learned how to allow ourselves to be overwhelmed, how to let go of control, how to go beyond the pain we have become so accustomed to. So we continue to examine our resistance to life, the ancient griefs that have so profoundly dulled our perception and limited our experience to just old pathways of silent desperation. In a very real way, when we are in grief, we are no longer so blind to our blindness.

It is at this stage of recognition, of acknowledgment, and the slow acceptance of the condition that we find ourselves in, that tenderness is most necessary. It is a tenderness that simply allows us to feel what we feel, the compassion with which we allow the process to unfold as it may.

Go slowly and with great gentleness into the dark night of the mind that's been confronted with loss, with all the losses that each loss puts us in touch with. Entering our grief directly, we see so clearly, perhaps as in no other process, our capacity to heal the past. Each loss offers us a remarkable opportunity of healing every loss. In every loss is recapitulated all previous losses.

Our grief is the reservoir of loss, a considerable pool of all the losses past and all the confusions present stored away without resolution. Often, from this deep underground pool of loss, feelings of helplessness and perhaps hopelessness arise. Our grief drains us and leaves us feeling only half alive, only partially able to heal.

We often wonder if we would feel the attenuated suffering called grieving if there were no residual grief beneath it all. It is not as though we wouldn't miss our loved one but instead might skip the middleman of the mind and go directly to the heart's sense of ever-connectedness.

Grief has the potential to allow us to see how cramped we have become. In acknowledging the pain, we can open past our long-held resistance to the unpleasant, to life itself. We dissolve old partiality into a new wholeness, able to let old pains be, to let them go, without clinging or suppression. This clears the way for life to reenter—a willingness, a non-condemning that allows the healing to go so deep. It means meeting "just this much" with mercy and awareness, recognizing that we don't need to change anything, but rather to add mercy and awareness to this moment so that what is can be as it is.

When we allow ourselves the feelings that arise around the loss of a loved one, we notice, unmistakably, a feeling of being distant from him or her. The first stage of grief is characterized by the experience of separation, of the loved one not being there, of the loved one's absence. Within that experience of separateness, one notices a quality created not only by death, but of our common daily grief. Many people have told us, "I am not sure if I am grieving their absence now or my absence then." At this point we may recognize that it is not just *our* feelings of separation but *the* feelings of separation—the common grief.

In many ways grief, in its initial impact, connects us to the place where separation always existed. It drops us into the mind, into that level where we thought that person more than experienced them. For instance, in the grief following the loss of our child, we may repeatedly imagine how we are not going to see that child grow up, how we are not going to see them get married, how we are not going to have grandchildren. If it is our lover, our spouse, our children, our dear friend who has been lost, we may feel how we are unable to share their growth, how we are not going to see them become what they had always wished to be. There is a profound feeling of not having. We can see how loved ones act as a mirror for our heart, how they allow us access to ourselves by reflecting back to us the love within. We see how they are a connection with the place within us that is love. When that loved one is lost, we grieve deeply the loss of connection with ourself.

So, in the early exploration of grief, we come across feelings of separation, a sense of "I and other." These have always been felt but seldom acknowledged, except when heavy states such as anger or fear or envy or doubt magnify the distance between the heart and mind. We come across the levels of remorse, of guilt, of self-doubt which may naturally follow. We are not taken by surprise but instead can watch each state in its unfolding, allowing deeper and deeper insight into the process. We can see that grief too has its own nature, its own tone of voice, its own texture, its own patterns in the body and tape loops in the mind. And hard as it may seem, we begin to make friends with our grief, and thus are reminded of how long we have forgotten, locked in our own little cage, reaching through the bars, hardly able to make contact with another. In this seeing we are set free. The past no longer compulsively creates the future, and we see yet another alternative to our suffering. We acknowledge with deep forgiveness how much self-mercy it takes to be fully alive and how difficult it is to live solely in the mind and still be able to breathe another into our heart.

As the process of grief deepens, as the mind begins to sink into the heart, we see the power of opening into our pain with mercy and awareness. It may take months, it may even take years. The heart has its seasons, and even as the mind sinks into the heart there may be times when we can touch our pain with care and tenderness, and times when once again the mind interposes its long-conditioned "shoulds" and tension and control.

As the mind sinks into the heart, there are moments when we feel how inseparable we are and have always been. Perhaps a sense of connection that existed even before we were born, a sense of the deathlessness of our essential oneness.

When the grief sinks so deeply into the heart that we can accept even this much pain and touch what a murdered girl's mother called "our shared divinity," we are healing to the core of life. Even though one may still feel terrible at times, the healing continues. We are not surprised at how little capacity we have at times to remain open, not surprised at how it changes, how our healing comes and goes. We notice how there may be moments or whole days of great openness and a deep sense of connection, but upon awakening the next morning we discover that the heart is seemingly inaccessible—a density where just a few hours before had been considerable spaciousness. As the healing discovers itself, drawing from beyond all previous resources and with unimaginable tenderness, we make room in our heart for ourselves even when our heart is closed.

At this stage of our grieving, of our healing, nothing can take that sense of beingness away. We are inseparable, and our connection is recognized beyond and before time.

Perhaps a greater tragedy than the loss of a child or the death of a dear friend is how often we feel this communion missing from those with whom we share our life.

For each and all of us, our work is to heal the grief that separates us from those we love so that we may begin to experience our wholeness and share it now in this moment.

For many, the healing that occurs through the exploration and recognition of grief does not begin until loss has arisen. But for some, there is a profound recognition of the "work that is to be done," to meet the pain now, the suffering now, finishing our business and allowing each moment to be new. Breaking the continuum of old pain, of old separation and grief that has often limited our experience of life, of ourselves and each other.

Meeting the grief in mind, meeting the grieving world with a bit more wisdom and forgiveness, we enter the healing moment fully alive.

THE MOTHER OF MERCY MEDITATION

(To be read slowly to a friend or silently to oneself.)

As the griefpoint becomes the touchpoint of the heart, *continue to feel the opening at the center of the chest and breathe into it.*

Focus on the breath of the heart.

Each inhalation drawing loving kindness through the griefpoint into the channel that leads to the heart. Each exhalation letting go of the pain.

Breathing mercy into that point. Breathing out the suffering, the holding, the armoring.

Let it all float in the boundaryless ocean of the heart.

Let the pain come. Let the pain go.

Let it float. No holding. No pushing it away. Just letting it be like a frightened child as it settles into the mother's warm embrace.

Breathing into the heart the mercy that is so much greater than our pain. The loving kindness that has room for it all, for our life, for our mind, in our heart.

Breathe loving kindness into the touchpoint of the heart.

Softening into the heart let the mind envision a loving presence in the room. A kindly being who cares for you with all her heart. It is the Mother of Mercy.

Feel her gentle approach, the whole belly softening to receive this blessing.

Soft belly.

Soft heart.

The arms of the Mother of Mercy are about you. All you need do is put your head on her shoulder.

All about her is a golden light.

Sense this light surrounding the Mother of Mercy. See it emanating from her magnificent heart. It is the light of the Great Heart of Compassion seen there before you, shining as kindness and care for your well-being.

Breathe that golden light into the touchpoint that goes beyond the pain. Breathe in the light.

Breathe out the shadow.

Shadows vanishing into the golden mist. The pain floating free in the heart of the Mother of Mercy.

Give it to her. She has room for it all.

Let your pain float in the heart of loving kindness.

In the warm embrace of the Mother, her mercy enters your heart like a rivulet of light. Becoming a stream. Becoming an ocean there in the center of your chest.

Flooding the body with light.

So much light expanding. Easing the holding, releasing the grief. Letting the healing in.

The past, like a wave vanishing into the still surface of this ocean of mercy and compassion.

Let the wave pass. Let go gently into the stillness.

The pain dissolving in the light.

The angry, frightened, hurtful past breathed out like dark fumes, dissipating in space.

Breathing in the light of healing, of mercy, of loving kindness.

Breathing out the smoky darkness of long smoldering griefs. Curly black wisps dissolving at the edge, absorbed into the light.

Letting go of the long-held pain with each exhalation.

Breathing in the golden aura of the Mother of Mercy.

Breathing out the dark smudgy pain. The armoring melting.

Let the golden mist that suffuses you dispel the hidden pain.

Breathe out the ancient suffering, breathe in the light.

Breathing out the shadow, let it go at last. No holding to suffering.

Letting go of our suffering is the hardest work we will ever do.

Breathe in the light, breathe out the pain.

Let the light in. Let the pain go.

Breathing out the holding, the merciless, the hidden pain, as the mind merges with the heart, healing our daily grief.

Grieved loved ones no longer lost in separation but merged inseparably in the heart.

All the parts of ourselves and all our departed dreams dissolving together into the light. So weary of the posturing and the pretense. So willing to come out of hiding. Let go at last into the vast shimmering spaciousness of your true nature, standing there before you in the guise of the Mother of Mercy.

Breathe her heart into your heart. Let your heart burst into hers.

Breathing the healing luminescence into the heart. Breathing out the unkindness, the dread, the unaccepted grief. Letting it all go at last.

Breathing the warm golden fire of her mercy directly into the heart.

The breath of love.

As you breathe in this light, the outbreath becomes paler and more transparent as we let go.

Holding released with each exhalation. Healing fed with each breath taken directly into the heart. Breathing in the divine mercy, the holding softens.

The out-breath getting clearer and clearer.

The in-breath and the out-breath equally filled with light.

The light drawn in brighter and brighter. A golden focal point at the center of the heart. The pain embraced by a deep confidence and merciful awareness.

As the out-breath clears an intensifying luminescence is brought in and sent out with each breath. We share the healing.

Gradually the light of mercy and compassion is breathed out toward all those in need. Sharing this healing with all grieving beings everywhere.

Breathing in the light. Breathing out the light.

Breathing the light to all beings everywhere. Sending loving kindness to sentient beings on every plane of existence.

Bathing their pain in the golden light of the Mother of Mercy. Breathing her deep kindness out to all those lost in the mind of pain and separation. Not grasping to their pain but letting it float in compassion and care. Breathing the light of healing back into their hearts.

May all beings be free of suffering.

May all beings' hearts be open to their pain.

The light flooding their shared heart.

Each heart encouraging the earth to heal.

Each exhalation carrying the light back to sentient beings everywhere.

May all beings be free of suffering.

May all beings be at peace.

May all beings dissolve the shadows of the past into the light of the healing present.

May we all live in mercy and care for each other and for ourselves.

May we all come to treasure ourselves and each other. And may we all come to treasure each other in ourselves.

WARMTH AND PATIENCE HEART BREATH

O nce the touchpoint of the heart is established, one can simplify the heart breath meditation into a warmth and patience breath practice. Breathing in and out of the heartpoint. Breathing in warmth. Slowly opening into patience on the out-breath.

Drawing in the rich warmth and mercy (of the Mother of Mercy). Cultivating patience. (Not waiting patiently. There is no such thing. One is either waiting or one is patient. Patience is a presence in the present.) As we slowly exhale.

As the grief meditation leads to the heart, the warmth and patience breath maintains that openness. And we begin to soften and liberate even our dull-eyed, everyday, ordinary grief. We open into the space in which liberation can occur.

Breathing in warmth.
Patience slowly, gently, on the out-breath.
Letting the healing in.
Letting go of suffering.

STEPPING OFF THE PATH

Practice, like life, runs in cycles. Sometimes one meditates daily. Sometimes one is too busy for life. Sometimes the heart is open. Sometimes it is not.

Meditation guides the mind into the heart. We are open for weeks or months or even years at a time. But our healing seems to be an upward spiral. We come again and again to the same teaching at another level. It is, as Buddha said, "The work that is to be done." Sometimes we open to that work. Sometimes we don't.

At certain times in our practice the work might become so difficult, the healing so deep, that we need to just sit down and look around. Sometimes we need a break before we continue on again.

Indeed, in a lifetime of practice there may be times when meditation recedes into the background noise of the needs and necessities of our life. And we worry we have "stepped off the path." But once you've committed to the heart, there is nowhere else to go. Though the forms may change you are always heading home.

Even though some people, particularly teachers who are attached to having students, may say you have "fallen out of grace," trust your process of growth, even when the old has fallen away and the new has not yet presented itself.

Part of the path includes the times we step off the path. Moments of integration and reflection. It gives perspective. "A chance to think," as they say. And to notice how unsatisfactory that too can be at times.

Stepping away from practice can also help us see that our life is not a method. That we are seeking liberation, not expertise in a craft. Recognizing how crafty we have become in spiritual technologies brings us back to what Zen master Suzuki Roshi called "beginner's mind." And we take our next step as "complete beginners." We reenter the path, recognizing that the object isn't to be a good meditator but simply to *be* with as much mercy and awareness as possible. Stepping off the path is often another step on the path.

In a lifetime of practice what the word "practice" means changes considerably. Practice is a process. To practice is to take each opportunity for wisdom, to pay attention. It is a clearing of priorities toward the truth.

OPENING THE HEART OF THE WOMB—A HEALING EXPLORATION

These are healing meditations. They began from the work that Ondrea and I shared for ten years with women who had been sexually abused.

In the course of a ten-day "conscious-living/conscious-dying" intensive, exploring the grief which we all share, it became quite evident that many of the women in that room experienced a profound grief that did not result from the death of a loved one. They grieved the loss of trust and comfort since being sexually abused.

After a particularly intense meditation, one woman stood up gleefully to share with the group her out-of-the-body experience during the meditation. Though that was not the intention of the meditation, occasionally such experiences spontaneously arise. She was glowing with her sense of being more than the body, of floating free of the dense, when another woman somewhat anxiously raised her hand. "I don't mean to interrupt but I have something very important to say." She stood. "You know, I think all of this out-of-the-body stuff is real nice, real showy, but I would like an in-the-body experience for a change! I would like my body to be a safe place to be, not a target. I would like my body to be home, but I never feel at home in my body because my body has been trespassed, vandalized. I've locked all the doors now and I can't get back in." Many women in the room began to sob for this shared truth that the body was simply not a safe place to be. Many working with illness wept as well.

After this very intense and incredibly moving session, a woman approached me and said, "You know, I have no more room in my heart now than I had in my body when I was two years old and my father raped me." And instantly it became clear, the connection between the upper heart and the lower* heart. And that many women had found access to the upper heart difficult because of the necessity to close the lower heart, the womb, the genitals, for self-protection, for survival. Often unable to take the next breath with any peace or assurance. It became clear that women have two hearts: the heart in the chest and the heart in the womb. And that from abuse to the womb heart, the "other heart," fear, distrust, anger, doubt, even self-hatred had limited access to the spaciousness and ease residing eternally in their upper heart.

And from her words, the Opening the Heart of the Womb Meditation arose as if from grace. It was inspired by the pain we all share. It allows us to participate in the healing for which we must all take responsibility. None of us are separate from the pain that any of us carry.

In the days when safe abortion was not legalized, women sometimes used a substance called ergot, a spas-

---

*"Lower" is not used here in any disparaging sense of a lesser degree of importance, but only to an anatomical reality.

modic for the smooth muscles of the body that could dislodge a pregnancy. But if the chemical was not perfectly titrated, perfectly adjusted to that person's weight and needs and metabolism, at times there would be heart palpitations. Because women have two major sets of smooth muscles in the body: the heart and the womb.

This meditation is based, as all healing is, on beginning to approach with mercy and loving kindness that which has been rejected by anger and fear, abandoned to helplessness. It is a rehabitation of the deserted and disheartened. It is a refilling with the light of the heart, the fearful womb. It is a deep mercy directed toward oneself. A profound letting go of the pain into a vast kindness, a merciful awareness.

As the practice spread among hundreds, perhaps thousands of women, many began to apply the meditation to other conditions in the lower heart. Some found that the meditation not only healed the mental pain residing there but also began to shrink fibroid tumors or decrease the effects of PMS (premenstrual syndrome). Some using their great genius for healing began to apply this process for unfinished business in the womb to the healing of the residual imprints (unexpected but nonetheless present) of abortion. Or to say good-bye and finish business after a hysterectomy. Some said it effected their cancer. Others to prepare, for an infant in utero, a smooth birth.

And at least a few have mentioned that it changed the nature of their infertility. The first of such healings was mentioned to us when a woman approached and said, "Stephen, I am pregnant and it's all your fault." Ondrea and I laughed. She had experienced eight miscarriages in the past ten years. When she sensed the meditation might be applicable "to make my womb a bit more hospitable for life," the practice helped her let go of some of the fear, some of the anger, and replace it with a new softness, a kindness, a newness she had never thought possible. Her healing went all the way back to her birth and to birth itself.

Though some speak in glowing terms of this practice, for many women who have been sexually abused, this may not be an easy meditation. Many women have told us that whether they work with this practice once a day, once a week or once a month, they find it the most difficult part of the day. And an indispensable aspect of their healing. It is not easy to approach such deep pain. It takes time, but what choice have we but to heal, to have mercy on ourselves and continue letting go of the enormity of the pain we carry.

This practice has grown from that single meditation (see "Great Injury" chapter of *Healing into Life and Death*), inspired by that woman's analogy of her heart to her womb, to a three-part progression. The healing of the heart of the womb personifies the very essence of the healing process. The acknowledgment. "The reversal of fortune" in which mercy approaches that from which fear has withdrawn. The profound entrance of mercy, the connecting of the heart with the disheartened. The letting go which is acutally the heart's enormous capacity to let be, the magic of our seemingly unworkable pain at last floating in something greater. And the sharing of this healing with all beings confronted with this same predicament.

The first step is the Healing into the Body meditation. It is a scanning of awareness through the body, beginning at the top of the head and progressing to the tip of the toes, focusing on area after area of sensation. It allows one to reenter the body with a new mercy, in a new safety, from a greater wholeness. This meditation may at first take anywhere from twenty to thirty minutes, depending on how each individual senses its application to their situation. If there is the slightest nuance that doesn't feel quite right, change it wholeheartedly to suit your needs. If the language doesn't fit or the pace isn't quite right, record these in your own voice or the voice of a lover, a loved one, so that it perfectly meets your needs, your healing. You are the path of healing and no one can liberate you so lightly, so mercifully, as your own perfect heart. Trust your own perfect intuition for what is right for you. Use these meditations as your own genius for healing indicates.

One woman mentioned that after working with body explorations (the Healing into the Body meditation), for many weeks, she still couldn't get below her eyes. That was as far as awareness was permitted to enter before an enormous wave of fear and resistance flattened her. So great was her distrust of reentering unsafe territory. I asked her how she could stand so much pain. And she said, "I can't. That's why I'm doing the meditation." What she was experiencing, even within the limitations of her great distrust, was that where a merciful awareness entered, healing was possible. She noted that where she had withdrawn awareness—due to fear or a sense of helplessness—a numbness, a deadness, was left behind. As she continued the practice, rejected parts of herself gradually became accessible. And in time she sensed a reintegration of her heart back into her body.

It can be difficult to guide mercy toward that which has been treated mercilessly. But the miracle is, even in this great pain, healing is possible. Hundreds have told us that these are among the most powerful tools they have found to "come back alive" into their body/mind. Bringing themselves back alive into life with a new trust and mercy for themselves and a care for all they love and loves them.

The second meditation is the Opening the Heart of the Womb practice. It is based on a very soft and merciful awareness, a gentle kindness that heals and strengthens whatever it embraces. It is the voice of your own heart reentering your own body, opening it gently to healing, moving tenderly through the vagina into the great dome of the womb, bringing moment-to-moment healing into the sensations there. Each sensation received with mercy and forgiveness and care. Filling with love that which had been pained by another's cold indifference. Healing the lower heart, finding greater access to the heart we all share. The heart of healing, the heart of compassion and mercy. In the Opening the Heart of the Womb meditation one needs go at their own pace, in their own way. Taking the meditation into their healing and encouraging others to do the same.

It is quite possible that no two people will do the meditation in exactly the same way. Each needing to hear so uniquely their own path, their own way into their own heart. Listening to the heart of their womb. Taking birth at last in the safety of loving kindness, in the sacred body of being.

One woman, after working with the meditation for a few months, said that although it was the "heaviest" part of her day, each day seemed a little lighter. Each day she discovered perhaps a millisecond more of trust, of self-love, of mercy. One morning while putting food out on the breakfast table for her children she looked up and saw the wall. "I just *saw* the wall," she said, tears pouring down her face. "It was a miracle, I was just there. There wasn't any fear, or doubt, or anger. I was just there—I just saw the wall. I didn't have to be *anywhere* else, *anyone* else, *anything* else. The room I stood in was my home. The world was my home at last." In the years that followed she helped many work with this meditation and find their own perfect way to their own perfect heart.

The last meditation, A Healing Shared, is a loving kindness meditation. It takes the healing work one is doing on oneself and begins to direct it toward all who are also in such pain. Although when we are in pain we may feel more alone than ever, in actuality we are part of an enormous lineage of suffering that is occurring at this same moment in thousands, tens of thousands, perhaps millions of other sentient beings who, too, long so not to suffer. Who also wish only to be at peace in this confusing and often violent world.

Many of the women working with these meditations have said that after a few sessions of sweeping through the body, reentering, they could go quite quickly to the second stage, the Opening the Heart of the Womb meditation. Having felt a certain reintegration, they found it took only a few minutes of opening into the body before continuing with this practice. Of course sometimes the mind was open, the body was soft and mercy was allowed, while at other moments they felt as though they had never done the practice before. This is just the nature of the ever-changing mind with its varying qualities of concentration and energy, patience and resoluteness. But when these qualities are balanced, they allow healing to be directed. From this inner directedness a sense of workability about life arises which was previously unimagined.

As one woman said, "If this is workable, anything is workable! I never thought I could make love again and now I make love to almost everything I see and hear. It has been so painful to go through this work and I have never been happier in my life."

If one is drawn to these practices it may be advisable to work closely with a therapist and/or someone you trust deeply and to whom you can speak from the heart in the process of shedding the pain and discovering your own enormous power for healing. If you are working with a therapist, you might consider sharing these meditations with them so they can get a sense of the method and how it works for you.

These meditations are still in the process of evolution. Only the heart knows best their application. Please use them for the benefit of yourself and all sentient beings. That is the joy of the third of these practices, the Healing

Shared in Loving Kindness Meditation. The mark of true healing is that we pass it on to others.

These meditations too seem very beneficial for the men who have worked with them. One man came up to us in tears after first attempting these meditations and said, "You know, I am not an abuser, I've never hurt or raped anyone. I am just a man with a male conditioning and these meditations have deeply moved me. I will never touch a woman carelessly there, unconsciously there, ever again." When men find their wombs they find a deeper place in their heart for women and for peace.

If this practice seems useful, perhaps you might want to refer to the "Great Injury" chapter in *Healing into Life and Death*. It offers an expanded sense of how others have approached this practice and their many variations on the theme.

Please make this practice your own and know that this healing is your birthright.

A NOTE ON THE HEALING INTO THE BODY MEDITATION

This Healing into the Body meditation allows a healing awareness to explore the body. It is a skillful way to begin the Opening the Heart of the Womb practice. It is a safe reentry into the body. Like any healing meditation it is a rehabitation of mercy and awareness into deserted areas of the body/mind.

Used for twenty minutes or more a day, many have noted a clearing from the body of long-held pains. And a softening of ancient hardness. It fills our deadspots with a new aliveness. It allows direct contact with the life-force.

This practice of flooding the body with a healing awareness, refined by mercy and self-forgiveness, allows direct reception of sensation. Then that contact with sensation becomes a conduit for the energies of the heart. We begin at last to take birth wholly. To touch the pain,

274

as well as those parts numbed by pain, with a new mercy, with a deeper healing.

Perhaps this is the alchemy to which Jesus referred when he suggested being reborn. That we need to take on life repeatedly. To begin again, again. To struggle to the surface (and to the depths) to take again a breath like that first breath of life. To be born again to life. To enter the body, to take birth, so as to heal ourselves and all sentient beings. To take a sacred breath, to be born beyond the pain. To become fully alive.

HEALING
INTO THE BODY
MEDITATION

(To be read slowly to a friend or silently to oneself.)

*F*ind a comfortable place to sit in a quiet room and settle into a chair or cushion.

Just feel what sits there. Feel this body your true nature inhabits.

Begin by bringing your attention to the very top of the head.

Just feel sensations begin to arise in awareness.

It may take a moment or two for awareness to gather there.

Allow awareness of sensation to explore the softness of the scalp against the skullcap.

As awareness settles into the body widen the range of inquiry. Receive the sensations generated by the soft scalp contacting the hard skull. Notice how these sensations follow the curve of the skull to form the whole head.

Allow awareness to move slowly into the brow. Whatever sensations are arising there at the forehead, feel them wholly, completely.

Feel how the brow spreads out to form the temples, the sides of the head.

Whatever sensation arises there, receive it in a soft willingness just to let it be.

Releasing any tension around the eyes, allow this gentle awareness to feel the eyes in their sockets, the bone that surrounds.

As awareness explores, these sensations move into the softness of the cheeks.

Feel the teeth within the mouth, sensing the teeth cradled in the gums.

Sensation arising moment to moment where even awareness is focused.

Notice how the tongue lies in the mouth. Is it pressed against the upper palate? Does it lay against the floor of the mouth? Is it curled against the teeth?

Receiving life in the body as sensation.

Meeting sensation after sensation, area after area, with a merciful awareness that enters life wholeheartedly.

Notice the tingling at the tip of the nose. The warmth, the softness of the lips.

Feel the muscles of the jaw begin to soften as they let life in with mercy and loving kindness.

Receive the sensations arising behind the ears. And the presence of the ears as well, at the side of the head.

Feel this whole face, this whole head, its soft flesh, its hard bone, its vibratory quality, places of warmth, maybe places of coolness noticed.

Nothing to create. Just receiving sensation as it is generated by the life-force in the body.

Allow awareness to receive the multiple sensations that arise in the various parts of the head and face as awareness proceeds down through the neck.

As awareness passes through the throat, let it soften yet more deeply to receive any tension noticed there. Perhaps dry fear or the thick knot of the long unsaid. Perhaps just open space. But notice any secrets buried there. The often swallowed-away anger and fear may be felt as some hardness.

Let the awareness which receives old pains be merciful and kind.

Again, nothing to create, just a gentle receiving of this body/mind which wishes so to be whole, to heal.

Attend to whatever closedness or openness is apparent in the throat. Let it be touched by a new mercy, by a kindness that sends a sense of well-being into the long uncared for, the often swallowed away, the armoring imprinted in this body of joy and pain.

Feel the weight of the head perfectly balanced on the willing muscles of the neck. And how perfectly the neck spreads out to form the shoulders.

Feel the long muscles that extend from the shoulder, sensations floating in a gentle comforting awareness which receives these shoulders, this bone and tissue, as living suchness, pulsating, vibrating with aliveness, the head suspended above. The arms supported below.

Feel how the shoulders support the arms and how the arms cradle the sides of the body.

Feel the strength in the shoulders, the musculature, the bones, the tendons that so readily allow that remarkable capacity for movement, for action, for service.

Feel sensation in the shoulders as it spreads out into the top of the arms and down through the biceps. Feel whatever sensations arise at the elbow.

Allow awareness to move through the forearm. Feel how this miracle of life extends down each arm, filling the palm, vibrating to the tip of each finger.

Feel how that vibrant quality animates the muscles, the tissue, the flesh that comprises the arms, the shoulders, the hands.

Allowing awareness to receive even the subtlest energy that arises, continue now down the other arm feeling the

shoulder, the forearm, the hand. Multiple sensations arising and dissolving, the life-force, received as moment-to-
moment sensation.

Exploring with mercy the field of sensation we call the
body.

Each arm alive with the suchness, the vibration of
being in a body, coming again to life to learn, to serve, to
be. Notice how these arms embrace this body.

Feel the chest rising and falling with each natural
breath. Not controlling the breath, just letting it be in soft
space.

Feel the breath breathe itself in trust, each breath
following the last effortlessly.

Feel the heart beating within. Feel the lungs gently
opening to receive life with each breath.

Breathe breathing itself in the vast field of sensation.

Feel the whole torso, the front, sides, back, the whole
body floating as sensation in awareness.

Notice that wherever awareness enters, life is to be
found.

Feel the varying densities of different areas of the torso,
warm here, perhaps cool there. Full of sensation in one
part, perhaps dull, almost sensationless in another. And in
yet another, pain, solidified fear, concretized doubt, setting
sensation afire, then flickering out in the cool light of a
merciful awareness. Where awareness is directed, healing
arises.

Feel here and there the pressure and release that awareness allows as it opens the body.

This miracle of body touched by the magic of a loving
awareness, of a clear mind, of an opening heart.

Now allow this gentle awareness to move through the
back, beginning at the top of the spine where the neck is
rooted in the back of the shoulders. Allow this healing
awareness to gradually move down the spine, receiving

each vertebra one after another, in loving kindness, moving very slowly to the base of the spine.

The wonder of spine supported so perfectly by the flat muscles of the upper back, extending down to the long lateral muscles of the lower back.

Feel the tissues, the sensations arising and dissolving in the flesh, in the bone, in the tissue of this miracle.

Let your attention move gently to the base of the spine, approaching with great awareness the lower torso.

Notice very gently whatever sensations, thoughts, or emotions that arise as the exploration of healing moves toward the lower torso. What feelings, if any, predominate as awareness enters lower into the body?

Now continue this same exploration of the torso by proceeding gently down the front of the body. Receiving the hard bones as they spread out like a protective canopy above the open softness of the stomach and belly. Allow the belly to soften, to receive healing.

In soft belly arises the possibilities of completion. Just feeling the breath breathing itself in soft belly.

The muscles rising and falling all by themselves with each breath, just life breathing itself in soft belly, just life continuing to heal itself.

Feeling this lower belly, the abdomen, again notice whatever subtle sensation or thought arises as awareness approaches the pelvic area. Whatever tensions or thoughts, whatever joy, whatever song, whatever fear, whatever quality of mind/body arises, let it be met by a gentle awareness that cares only for its healing.

Touching the fear, the judgement, the doubt, the anger, with a new mercy. Letting life in, allowing for the possibility of healing.

Letting the healing in, let whatever sensations arise in the pelvic area be received in this merciful awareness.

Feel this whole area in softness and mercy. No force, no rush here, just a gentle allowing of sensations to present themselves as they will. There is no urgency. Awareness heals all by itself as it enters yet subtler and subtler levels of our holding, of our injury.

Completion gradually arises as awareness of feelings of incompletion are met in this softness, this non-judging heartfulness.

An awareness that meets the pain of mind and body with a new caring, with a loving kindness, and a sense of its own great power to heal. The healing which is our birthright.

Soften the lower belly, softening the hips, softening the buttocks. Allow this gentle awareness to move through, passing tenderly through the genitals to continue on into the upper legs down through the thighs, receiving the knee as sensation, the calves as vibration. Sensations of pressure, sensations of coolness or of heat, of roughness or smoothness simply experienced as they are in the heart of the moment.

As awareness moves through the legs down to the soles of the feet, one leg at a time, slowly, at your own pace, receiving the sensations of the body, awareness has just opened through. Feel the strength and durability of the legs and knees, the ankles and feet, the capacity of movement, the preciousness of each step they are able to provide.

Feel the vibration in the lower body. Feel both legs now, both feet, knees, hips, as an aliveness, a presence in the body.

Feel the rootedness with the earth at the bottom of each foot.

Feel trust growing at the bottom of each foot. Gratitude for this opportunity, even in the midst of such hard lessons, opens the heart, to become fully alive moment to moment.

Feel now this whole body as the field of sensation, a tingling, an aliveness of being, whole body filled with vibrating suchness.

Sensation touched by awareness and mercy. Each moment of sensation filled, flooded, with loving kindness.

Feel this whole body becoming one with the heart.

Feel how the areas of intense sensation and the areas of lesser sensation begin to connect with each other. Each part feeding the other. An osmosis of loving kindness where that which is needed is provided by itself in kindness and care. The heart illuminating the whole body, each sensation shining like a star in a dark sky.

The light of being shimmering in this healing body. In this body of mercy and service. In this body of loving kindness and awareness. In this body that wishes life and healing to all others who feel these same pains in this same moment.

May we all be free of suffering, may we all take from our pain a new healing that brings us beyond pain, beyond suffering to the heart of our true nature, to the birthright of our healing and wholeness.

May all beings be free of suffering.

May all beings be at peace.

A NOTE ON THE HEART OF THE WOMB MEDITATION

This meditation is the heart of this healing practice. It is that aspect most internalized and repeated. For some its personal variation has become a life companion—a key to the door to liberation.

One woman, working with it a few weeks, noticed that some areas were more difficult than others to gain healing access to and needed special attention. Using her intuition for healing, she re-created the meditation in her own image and likeness, in her own voice, adding special emphasis to the areas that she found most in need of attention. She "altered it to fit" her own special needs. She brailled her way toward her heart. She allowed her life to be an experiment in truth.

OPENING THE
HEART OF THE
WOMB
MEDITATION

(To be read slowly to a friend or silently to oneself.)

In a safe, quiet space find a comfortable place to sit and settle in there as you let your awareness begin to come to the level of sensation in this body.

Just feel what sits here.

Feel the multiple sensations arising and dissolving in the body, tinglings here and there.

Feelings of warmth or coolness.

Feelings perhaps of the pressure of the buttocks on the cushion on which you sit.

Let awareness come to the multiple shimmerings and movements of the field of sensation we call the body.

And begin to direct the awareness toward the area where the legs meet.

Gradually awareness gently gathers there at the inner thigh, at the place where the upper leg meets the body.

Very gently now, awareness receiving sensation arising in this very tender, very powerful area of life, of birth, of being.

Just receiving very tenderly whatever sensations are generated there and noticing too whatever feelings, emotions arise in the approach toward this sacred area.

Allow this soft awareness to receive the sensations at the labia. Meet each moment of sensation with a mercy and care that pours from the heart into the body.

Feel this sacred place of power experienced as sensation floating in a merciful awareness, in a tenderness, absorbing moment to moment each sensation arising.

Allow awareness to gather as it will without the least sense of urgency. Allow a merciful exploration of this area.

Feel the ruffled fringe of flesh that protects this tender area. Just allowing awareness to gather there gently with a healing mercy, receiving sensation moment to moment in a deepening softness and self-care.

Tenderly moving through the shadows and light into the area of the vulva.

Feel the muscles there as strength, their power, their wholeness.

Notice the multiple sensations that arise as awareness receives the vagina. Let them float in a healing mercy that receives the moment in loving kindness and a new strength.

Feel the light of awareness filling the holy body of the vagina.

Gently, gently allowing the light of your mercy to illuminate this moist, merciful cradle of life, of love, of healing.

Touching so tenderly the subtle wrinkles, as well as the powerful muscles of the vagina.

Let the vagina fill with your kind light, a soft glow brightening moment to moment with each sensation received there. The healing melting away whatever pain, whatever fear may reside there.

Allowing awareness to soften and receive life as it fills

the body. Allowing mercy to merge with the sensations that arise in the vagina.

A merciful awareness moving so tenderly into the cervix and muscles. The tissues softening to receive this healing mercy, this light expanding into the great dome of the womb.

The womb filling with golden light, with infinite mercy and compassion for itself.

The light illuminating the cave of life, the sacred womb.

Feel its spaciousness, its openness, its homeness.

Let awareness receive the womb with mercy and loving kindness for yourself, for this tender heart.

Let your womb fill gradually with this golden light shining from your mercy, lighting and lightening this heart of life and being.

Let the heart of the womb open to receive its own great nature once again, to come home to itself, to make room for you in this great womb heart.

Let the soft light of that heart shine there, opening the womb of mercy, of forgiveness, of compassion for yourself.

Letting the womb soften, let its heart open.

Letting it just be at last in loving kindness, in a gentle healing mercy.

And sense the fallopian tubes extending like branches from this sacred tree of life. The living trunk of the vagina extending through the cervix, spreading into the canopy of the womb, its branches like arms embracing itself.

Feel the loving kindness, slowly expanding in the womb, flow into the fallopian channels through which all life has passed.

Allow the light of the womb to move gradually into each of the great branches on the tree of life.

Allow the light of this great heart to bring mercy to itself, to heal itself in loving kindness, to allow itself its own embrace, its own fulfillment, its own completion.

Feel the warm golden light, flowing through the branches of the tree, entering as light into the ovaries. Shimmering in each seed within.

Feel the whole tree of light, of life, filled with its own healing power. Filled with tender mercy.

Feel the feathery ends of the fallopian tubes and the shining fruit at the end of each branch. The whole womb healing into a new mercy and self-kindness, filling with tender care.

Let the womb fill with love for itself and for all sentient beings everywhere.

As the heart gradually sinks into the womb, the upper heart and the lower heart merge to form the shared heart.

The upper heart and lower heart forming a single shimmering star, the shared heart of being, the heart of completion.

Let it be. Let the healing dissolve whatever pain remains in a new joy, in a new sense of our own great power to heal and to be at last.

Let the heart sink into the womb receiving itself in wholeness and mercy and joy.

As the light of healing suffuses the womb, receiving moment to moment each sensation and feeling in a profound gratitude for healing, sense all the other women who at this very moment also long to be free of the pains of the past. And let the light from the heart of the womb radiate out into the world, sharing this healing with all who now wish so to be free of these same pains and fears.

Let the light from the heart of your womb flood this world of pain and confusion, sharing this healing with all other beings.

As the light in your womb intensifies let it expand out to all the other wombs, all the other women everywhere who share this same path of healing, who too at this moment take birth anew.

Share the healing with all who reach out for completion.

Allow the light to be.

May we all be free of a past of pain and confusion.

May we let our wombs, our hearts, be filled with their own natural light.

May we be whole unto ourselves.

May we be at peace.

May all beings be free from suffering.

May all beings know the joy, the healing, of their true lumincescent nature.

May we all meet in mercy, in non-injury, in compassion.

May we be healed.

May we be at peace.

May all beings be free.

May we all be free.

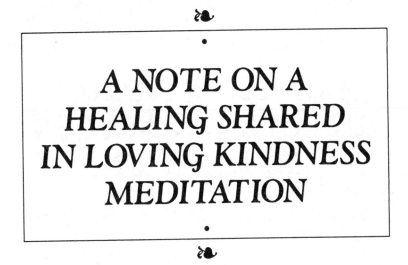

A NOTE ON A HEALING SHARED IN LOVING KINDNESS MEDITATION

Sharing the healing, or what Buddhists call "sharing the merit," is the final stage of healing. It is also the first stage of being healed. Clearly, loving kindness is the beginning and end of this process of completion.

This meditation is a variation on the loving kindness meditation with which this book was begun. It also develops the heart breath developed in the final stages of the grief meditation. It is among the most powerful of our healings—more than simply removing pain, it approaches the end of suffering. It integrates the mind into the heart. It allows us to take a sacred breath. It cultivates a sense of the shared sacred.

•

A HEALING SHARED IN LOVING KINDNESS MEDITATION

•

(To be read slowly to a friend or silently to oneself.)

*F*ind *a comfortable place to sit and settle in there.*
Let the body soften.
And let your attention come to the heart.
Let each breath be drawn into the heart.
Let each exhalation release the pain there.
So much holding, so much armoring around the heart.
So much life unlived, unloved there.
As you breathe into the heart, feel the mercy enter.
Slowly the heart begins to fill with loving kindness.
We carry such pain, such judgement, such unkindness
for ourselves.
   Let the breath of the heart dispel the pain. As you
breathe in say in your heart, "May I be happy, may I be
free of suffering, may I be at peace."
   As you gently let go of the breath, exhaling, say, "May
my pain be healed, may I enter the joy of my true nature
beyond even this longing to be free."

"*May I be free of suffering. May I be happy. May I be at peace.*"

Each breath drawing into itself a sense of well-being, a wish for one's own healing and completion.

May I be happy. May I be at peace. May I be free of suffering.

Let the heart look upon you as if you were your only child. Let it direct toward you feelings of well-being. Let it embrace you. Let yourself in.

Breathe yourself into your heart in mercy and loving kindness.

Notice whatever old mind discontent tries to block this: the self-judgement, the distrust, the mercilessness with yourself—let it be breathed out, let it be displaced by this loving kindness that each breath draws into the heart.

May I be happy.

May I heal the anger, the judgement, the pain, the indifference. My forgetfulness.

May I be free of suffering.

May I be at peace.

Each breath softening the body, clearing the mind, opening the heart.

Each breath healing us back into ourselves, into our boundaryless beauty, into the edgeless vastness of our true nature.

May I be happy.

May I be free of suffering.

May I be at peace.

Allowing yourself to let go of all that blocks your entrance into the heart, all that blocks your birthright of healing and mercy and loving kindness.

Each breath drawing in the healing.

Each exhalation releasing the pain, the armoring.

Peace comes into the heart like the morning sun spreading across the ocean. It is the ocean of compassion. It is the bright light of mercy flooding the heart. Welling over into the body. *The whole body softening in mercy and loving kindness. Embracing yourself.*

Have mercy on you.

Let the love in.

Let yourself be healed into your own forgiveness and loving kindness.

And recognizing that just as you wish to be happy, so do all beings everywhere; begin to send this healing kindness, this loving mercy out to another. Perhaps a dear friend, a loved one, a mate, a beloved person in your life, touch them now. Send to them now this same wish for their well-being that you are absorbing into your body for your own deep healing.

Let them float in this ocean of compassion that is your heart.

Let this loved one be immersed in your loving kindness.

And breathing into your heart, draw in the mercy, a concern for their well-being and breathe it back out to them. Silently saying, "May you be happy, may you be free of suffering, may you be at peace. Just as I wish to be happy, so I know do you. May your life be filled with light and loving kindness and forgiveness for yourself and all others. May you be free of suffering, may you be at peace, may you be happy."

Drawing this loving kindness into your heart, send it directly back to them. "May you be healed of whatever pain blocks your heart. May your life move toward healing each day in compassion and care. May you be happy. May you be free of suffering. May you know the absolute joy of your absolute nature. May you be healed into the peace that is our birthright."

Each breath sending energy into their heart, filling them with your loving kindness. Filling them with your care and kindness.

And let this love extend to everyone in the house in

which you sit now or the room in which you find this
meditation growing in your heart.

Let this loving kindness radiate to all you love and care
for.

May all these beings be free of suffering.

May all these beings be filled with the luminescent
happiness of their original nature. May they be healed into
the peace we all seek.

And continue expanding this loving energy. Let it
radiate from the heart until it encompasses everyone in the
city, in the state where you live.

Embracing equally all in pain. All those whose heart
cannot yet see. All those whose pain is too great to sense
the possibility of healing. Breathing mercy to all beings in
suffering. All those so in need of love, so in need of
healing.

Let them be encompassed by the radiance of your heart.
May all beings be free of suffering.

The whole planet floating like a bubble on the ocean
of compassion which is your heart.

May all beings be free of suffering.

May all experience the openheart of their miraculous
nature.

May they be free of suffering.

May they be at peace.

The whole world like a bubble floating in the ocean of
compassion that is your heart.

May all beings be healed into the light of their joy, of
their mercy, of their loving kindness.

May all beings be free.

May all beings be free of suffering.

May we all open to the shared heart, the one heart
experienced by all.

And continue this expansion of loving kindness,
breathing all beings into your heart in mercy, in healing
kindness, in completion, in peace.

Let this loving kindness expand into every plane of reality, seen and unseen.

May all beings, no matter what form they take, no matter what pain assails them, be free of suffering.

May all beings be blessed, from the ancient saints to those yet to be born, may all be at peace.

May all beings be free of suffering.

May they receive the healing they take birth for.

May all awaken to the true heart's release.

May all beings everywhere be free of suffering.

May all beings everywhere be at peace.

BE YOUR OWN FOOL

Be your own fool. Trust your process. No one knows what needs be done for your healing better than you. Kabir says we have ways within each of us which will never be known by anyone. Trust those ways. You are the path.

Don't be someone else's fool—Buddha's, Mary's, Moses'—tread yourself lightly.

The comparing mind often attempts to adjust the compass, to navigate by another's stars. And we become lost.

Even Buddha's disciples each had to find their own way through the teachings. One monk, who tended to lose mindfulness of speech when leaving the monastery on alms rounds, used his own genius for healing and took a bit of water in his mouth and held it there until he returned with his begging bowl full. If he started to lose mindfulness and began to unconsciously mention the beauty of a flower or a tree, the involuntary mechanism of swallowing would occur and as the water disappeared from his mouth he would stop right where he was to sit down and meditate and wait for the rest of the monks to go to town and return. He found his own path. As did another monk on those same alms rounds who noticed that he would lose mindfulness when walking. So he held a pebble under his toes knowing that if he should become distracted by a beautiful bird or desire for food his toes would automatically drop the stone, which instantly brought him to his senses. (Clearly our meditation is most called for when we are not on our cushion. When we are in our daily lives treading our life path.) Each of these beings, though exposed to one of the great teachers, had to discover some way peculiar to their own nature to apply these teachings.

For each of us to apply what we sense is right, we need become God's fool. We need be open at the edge to all that might arise. Beyond the rational, in the heart of the matter, allowing the mystery to dance with an intuitive sense of the appropriate. Perhaps beyond anything we have "known" before.

More than once I have gone out on a limb to make contact with a dying patient in a manner which might have seemed quite foolish to anyone else in the room but which found its way to the heart of the patient. Various examples of such foolishness are available in our previous books.

To be your own fool you need to eat the judging mind and surrender it to God, or the great "don't know," whichever comes first. Comparing mind is judging mind. It does not trust the ground beneath its feet. It wants to be better than it is thus never knowing its joyous immensity. Imagining that one state of mind is preferable to another, seldom recognizing the vast satisfaction in which even the unsatisfactory floats.

Our friend Wavy Gravy used to volunteer as God's fool in a children's cancer ward. He would enter in clown garb with enormous plastic scissors and a big red nose and say to the children in a shrill voice, "I've come to take out your stitches!!!" and the children would laugh and invite him close. And he would sit on their beds and listen and touch, and when they cried he would eat their tears. He was the "lightness of being" in tap shoes. He was Nobody's Fool.

Jesus said you need not distort your face in order to know God. But for many spiritual aspirants there is a kind of constipation born of fear and a sense of not-enoughness, which limits their progression. They are trying so hard to be soft, but force closes the heart. Indeed, it takes hard work to "let go lightly," but there is such joy in the process.

Are you enjoying it?

Spiritual work calls for spiritual play. Perhaps the 10 percent nonsense Aldous Huxley suggested as an essential part of growth. And not to make nonsense a serious business like the workshop participant who asked, when the 10 percent figure was mentioned, "Is that a minimum or a maximum?" I couldn't answer the question. It seems always to change.

Nonsense and loving kindness are exquisite playmates for the serious work of healing. Play softens the body and opens the heart's throat. It lets us sing our song as we remember it, to "make a joyous sound" and dance in the fields of the spirit.

Be your own fool. Walk nobody's path but your own. Trust your vision. Be a lamp unto yourself.

MAY THIS BE YOUR LAST BIRTHDAY
An Experiment in Consciousness

As a new student, during one of my first long meditation retreats, I returned to my room on my birthday to find a note from the teacher on the pillow which read, "May this be your last birthday." I was a bit confused by this, and thought, "Wow, this practice requires more than I imagined!" But then I realized the wish was a blessing, not a curse. It was reminding me of the unborn and deathless quality of our true nature.

We celebrate the physical body each birthday. When we say, for instance, "I am twenty-five years old," what speaks is the "I am," which identifies itself as the body. That is our fear of death. A case of mistaken identity.

The "I" celebrates bodies and birthdays. But "am-ness" is an ongoing celebration of our original nature.

Don't take your next birthday so personally. Take a year off. Rejoice in life rather than just your tiny body.

When we begin to celebrate the Real Body, we no longer blow out the candles, but gather all separate flickerings into a single brilliance which causes the heart to burst into flame and the mind to become clear space.

It is by this singular light that we explore that which existed before we were born and survives our death. Being-ness itself.

"I" blows out the candles. Am-ness is the breath. And love, is the breath inside that breath.

Lightly, my darling, lightly, even when it comes to dying. Nothing ponderous or portentous or emphatic. No rhetoric, no tremolos, no self-conscious persona putting on its celebrated imitation of Christ, or Goethe, or Little Nell. And, of course, no theology, no metaphysics. Just the simple fact of dying and the fact of the clear light.

—A. Huxley

CONSCIOUS DYING

Perhaps the first insight in the study of conscious dying is that the acknowledgment, opening, and letting go that is suggested is nothing new. It is "just this much" all over again. Big surprise!

The second is that we are not the body.

And the last is that we are simply awareness itself—momentarily disguised as "creation in the act of becoming."

It is a short course, but a hard curriculum. It means nothing short of taking birth at last. Opening to the labor pains. Accepting that first breath. And allowing the last. Clearly conscious dying is simply a personification of conscious living. No difference.

We have a body but it is not who we are. Just as you have an overcoat, but that is not you. One honors the overcoat as a given of the moment and because it would be quite unsatisfactory to revile it or let it go to rags when it could allow one to continue on one's long winter journey of wisdom and love. When it is spring, one does not need the overcoat anymore. One puts it aside or sends it to the cleaners.

At this point in this book, having practiced certain of the awareness exercises and perhaps getting a glimpse, a sense, of some deeper enormity underlying this mind/body process, the heart may well acknowledge that a deepening awareness of awareness itself, a broader consciousness of being, is the ideal practice for conscious living as well as conscious dying. Same thing.

Just as death is an illusion we all seem to buy into, so we must recognize that even such high-minded concepts as "conscious dying" can become a still greater trap if it creates a model of who, or how, we *should* be. Anything, even the idea of "going to God," can become a hindrance if it even subtly reinforces the tendency toward grasping at the next moment.

We hear of the death of Zen masters, of saints, of those we imagine are "remarkable people," dying without much resistance, and it seems as though all this may be beyond us. But death, like anything that catches the heart's attention, can bring out the best in us. We have seen many people, as they approach even the confusion around death, go beyond that dismay and become one with the process. They seem to go through what could almost be called "incarnations" in the last few months of their life. They deepen the work they perhaps took birth to complete. They are no longer someone separate, someone "dying consciously." They are merely space within space, light within light.

INTRODUCTION TO
DYING MEDITATION

As Walt Whitman wrote, "To die is different from what anyone supposes, and luckier." And simpler too.

Although the approach to life's end may indeed be difficult, painful, confusing, the end of this "end game" has a much different quality.

Death is a process of expansion. It is a progressive release from the dominance of the qualities that compose all substance. The earth, water, fire, and air characteristics of matter referred to in ancient sacred literature as well as many wholistic healing methods. The stages of dying are the stages of going from solidity to spaciousness. Each step of the process is one of greater expansiveness.

In the first stage of dying, after you've taken your last breath, the earth element, the experience of solidity in the body, begins to dissolve. Thus the first aspect noticed by one watching this process is that solidity no longer predominates; the person is immobile. This is the outer experience of someone viewing death, but it is not the inner experience of one dying. The inner experience is one of not being limited by the dense. The internal experience, as someone said, is like taking off a shoe that's too tight.

As feelings of solidity dissolve, and pain is no longer experienced, the water element, the quality of fluidity, asserts itself to create a sense of increasing flow and gracefulness.

As the fluid quality of the life-force, no longer limited to the solid body, is increasingly experienced, there is a sense of profound smoothness, even joy.

In this inner sense of fluidity one feels more like an ocean than a boulder.

Ironically, in the eyes of the joyless beholder all that externally marks this stage is that the circulation has ceased completely. For the loved one who stays with the body lying on its back, there is noticed the settling of a considerable amount of blood as the back becomes deep red.

It is perhaps at this point in the process that one realizes no one dies alone. Indeed, the movement of death from the separate to the universal is in precisely the opposite direction of that which causes loneliness. Every stage of dying is an increasing sense of moving toward greater and greater spaciousness.

It is quite noticeable here that the external characteristics of less and less to relate to, which we lament, are quite different than the internal experience of more and more of ourselves to respond from—an expansiveness for which we have always felt such gratitude. Obviously the nature of the physical body, the heavy body, is quite unlike that of the body of awareness, the body of light within. The physical decays as the spirit continues its pilgrimage.

As the water element dissolves into the fire element, that which heated the body and "fired the senses," the internal experience is one of a shimmering radiance like that which we see rising on a summer's day from a macadam roadway. The fire element is not a flame. It is the radiance that remains when the heat is removed. Indeed, as with all these progressive expansions, this sense of radiance, of shimmering spaciousness, increases a sense of equanimity which makes this experience not at all unpleasant.

The external experience of this dissolution into the heat element is of course that the body cools. If one has had the opportunity to be with a loved one after their death one may notice, by placing a hand on the dead friend's heart, that the heat remains in the heart long after it has dissipated from the rest of the body.

The internal experience is one of floating, of more and more space, of less and less edge. Moving from the separate toward the universal. From the limited to the unlimited.

As you can imagine, the inner experience of these stages is one of relief and an expanded sense of ease. The fears which have been maintained so long to protect this body, fall away with the notion of some body to protect. The heat element then dissolves into the air element. And we experience directly the lightness of being, the breath inside the breath released from breathing.

As the air element predominates, one experiences oneself as space dissolving in space. The tendency toward holding floats free. And mind is seen in the same way as the body from which we have just departed. Simply an accumulation of personal history, a moment in the past. And the past floats in the enormous present.

The external view of this stage is one of inert heaviness paled by the loss of the life-force. Again the external heaviness belies the internal lightness.

And then it is said that all elements dissolve into consciousness itself. This is the stage of the Great Light to which so many holy books refer. One directly experiences "that the many of the mind" are each aspects of the oneness of the heart.

It might be mentioned here that in all the tales we have heard of near-death experiences where one has left their body, perhaps even viewing it from above, and gone on toward further realms to meet the Great Light, very few have recognized that the light was their own true nature. The Great Light is yourself. It is our ordinary diffuse consciousness focused to a single pointed brilliance. Like the widely dispersed winter sun through a magnifying glass, it becomes a single blaze capable of igniting the cold world.

Even after death we meet ourselves and seldom recognize our enormity. So what else is new?! It is as Kabir says, "What is found now is found then." To the degree we honor our sacred light now we may be able to recognize it then. We keep mistaking our true nature for Buddha, for Jesus, for Mary, for Sareda Devi. It is another case of mistaken identity. We trade ourselves too small. When Jesus said, "I am the Light," he referred to the "I am" of pure being, the light itself. It excludes no one, no thing.

An apt analogy for the process of dying are the stages an ice cube goes through when it is placed in a warm room. In its original form it seems very solid, its edges are well defined in form. Its hardness, its solidity, are the predominant qualities noticed.

And then it starts to melt. The edges become less defined. The fluid element overwhelms the solid. The solidity falls away and the fluidity dominates. It becomes a puddle of water. That puddle of water is part of a process. As the liquid form spreads on the table, the quality of its heat element changes. It becomes room temperature. And begins to evaporate. Which means going from the liquid, the water element, to the air element, its gaseous form. Eventually, as with any gas, it fills its container equally in all its parts.

Clearly the essence of this material, H_2O, has not changed in the least. Only its forms have altered through a natural process. The essence never changes, only the forms it inhabits.

Imagine, particularly if you were ill or aged, how wonderful this process might be. A feeling of relief from the density of the pain of the physical body. A sense of fluid edgelessness melting in space. Of extraordinary space dissolving into itself. Light dissolving into light. No problem. A profound sense of liberation. And imagine approaching the Great Light aware of your divinity, recognizing that light as your own great nature. Imagine the sense of relief and wholehearted joy. Imagine being so prepared for your enormity, your power, your beauty that when it arises you don't attribute it elsewhere, and merge wholeheartedly. No separateness, no separation. What a healing!

Perhaps the extraordinary easy-mindedness and open-heartedness we hear about from so many who have had near-death experiences is attributable to the fact that at the time of death one's concentration becomes ten to fifteen times increased. That common light uncommonly focused. Not changing the nature of the light, simply experiencing its concentrated nature. No wonder there is such great calm. Calm is a by-product of concentration. The whole process so natural, so life affirming.

Indeed, the book *Who Dies?* is based on this investigation. If one is drawn to go beyond becoming only who we wish we were, and investigate, explore the miracle of who we have always been, these meditations may be very useful.

When we take death within, life becomes clear and workable. One of the remarkable things about confronting death is the depth to which it "catches our eye." The art of being fully alive is the art of catching our attention. It is awareness that frees us, not the object of awareness. If we could fully experience even a moment of just being in its totality, we would discover what we have always been looking for. If we would pay as much attention to the toast popping out of the toaster as we do to death we would be liberated much more quickly.

These meditations have been employed widely by those who are dying as well as by those helping a loved one prepare for death. And yet more important than preparing us for death is their capacity to focus us on life. To let go of the last moment and to open to the next is to die consciously, moment to moment.

In a sense, all of this talk about death is really a ploy. Because what we think of as death only occurs to the body. It threatens our seeming existence only to the degree we imagine and pretend it does. But because death catches our eye, focusing on it is a skillful means of becoming more alive. Wherever the attention is, wherever awareness is, that is where our aliveness is.

When we are fully alive we go beyond even death. Entering the spaciousness of being in which death too floats. It is like entering a room only to find it has no walls, no door, no one inside. Awakening from a dream to find we were never asleep (that sleep too was just part of the dream). It is going beyond creation and destruction. You are neither the dancer nor the dance. Nor even the ground on which the dance is played out. Nor the music. Nor the electrons or the space between them, not even the perception of them, nor the consciousness that you are none of them, nor the feelings that meet this recognition. Nor even the "don't know" that has allowed you to navigate this far. You recognize that you can't know who you are, you can only be it.

When we become the life-force itself, beingness, we go beyond even The Wheel of Birth and Death. We go beyond the limited comprehension of the mind, to the enormous intuition of the heart. Being never dies, only the forms it temporarily inhabits. All survive death. Death is just a change in lifestyles.

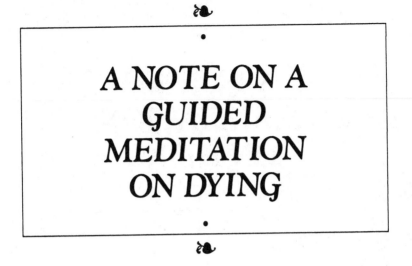

A NOTE ON A GUIDED MEDITATION ON DYING

Before you begin this meditation look about your home for a place to die. Go from room to room surveying the ambiance and sensing if you had to come home to die where in the house, how in the house, that might be best provided. Go to the place in your home where you might choose to die and just for the work/play of it, sit there to experiment with the meditation.

Later, as the meditation becomes more your own, you will be able to die anywhere.

A GUIDED
MEDITATION
ON DYING

(To be read slowly to a friend or silently to oneself.)

*F*ind a comfortable place to sit and let your eyes close.

Bring your attention to the level of sensation. Feel this body you sit in.

Let the body be still.

Focus on the sensation of being in a body.

Notice the body's substantial quality.

Feel the solidity of the body. Feel its weightiness, how gravity pulls on its substance.

Receive this quality of solidity.

Feel the weight of the head resting on the neck. Feel the musculature of that neck, its strength, its thickness.

Feel the long bones of the shoulders and the thick bony sockets that support the weight of the arms.

Feel the heaviness of the arms as they rest on either side of the body. Feel these heavy hands.

Feel the torso, its thickness, its weightiness. The earthen quality of this body.

Feel this heavy body in which you live.

Notice the solidity, the density, the earth element, of the dense body.

The pull of gravity as the buttocks are drawn into the cushion or the chair, as the feet press against the floor.

Notice gravity's action on this earthen body.

In this solid body, sensations arise. Tinglings, hot and cold, rough and smooth, soft and hard. Sensations arising in the body.

Recognize this flickering field of sensation.

Don't grasp at sensation. Just allow these sensations to be received as they arise in this body we inhabit.

Open to the sensations in the legs, their density, heaviness. Feel the solidness of this body.

Explore this container for the life-force.

And explore the life-force as sensation arising and passing away.

And as you note these sensations, notice how though they arise in the heavy body, they seem to be received by something subtler within. Something lighter within this heavier form.

Within this heavy body is a body of awareness, a light body which experiences hearing, seeing, tasting, touching, smelling, received through the outer body.

Feel the body of awareness, this inner body, this light body, perfectly nestled within the heavier form, receiving experience—experiencing.

Sense the lighter body within. The body of awareness that experiences all that enters through the senses. It recognizes sound as hearing. It delights in music. It experiences images as seeing. And recognizes great beauty. It experiences food as taste. It knows it is alive.

Enter this light body of awareness.

Observe how each breath drawn in through the nostrils of the heavy body is experienced as sensation by the light body, by the awareness within.

Notice how each breath connects the heavy body with

the light body. Each breath maintaining the light body within.

Each breath allowing life, awareness, to remain in the earthen vessel.

Observe the light body receiving the heavy body.

Feel this contact between the heavy body and the light body that each breath allows. Feel how each breath sustains the light body balanced perfectly within.

Breathe the connection between the outer body and the inner body drawn in as air, received as sensation. Each breath so precious. Each breath maintaining the connection, allowing life to remain in the body.

Feel how the breath connects the solid body with the light body.

Experience each breath.

Just awareness and sensation. Each breath. Experience this delicate balance, moment to moment, as sensation, as awareness itself.

And take each breath as though it were the last.

Experience each inhalation as though it were never to be followed by another.

Each breath the last.

The last breath of incarnation.

Let the breath come. Let the breath go.

The last breath of life leaving the heavy body behind.

Each breath ending. The connection severed between the heavy body and the light body.

The end of a lifetime. The final breath.

Each breath the last.

Let go. Don't hold on to it.

Let each breath go, finally and forever. Don't even be attached to the next breath.

As the last breath leaves go with it. Don't hold on. Let yourself die. Let the light body float free now.

Let yourself die.

Let go now.

Gently, gently, let it all go. Let it all float free. Let yourself die.

Leave the body behind and follow the light into luminous space.

Go into it. Let yourself die into space.

Each breath vanishes. Each thought dissolving into space. Don't hold now. Just let go once and for all. Let go of fear. Let go of longing. Open to the wonder.

Let yourself die. Open into death. Nothing to hold to. That is all past. Die gently into this moment.

Holding on to nothing, just let yourself die.

Let go of your name. Let go of your face. Let go of your reputation. Float free into the vastness.

Leave the body behind. Moving into the vast space of being.

Light dissolving into light. Just vast luminous space. Let go now. Have mercy on you, let yourself float free.

Merging with space. Space dissolving in space. Light dissolving in light.

Vast, boundaryless, space, expanding into space.

Such enormous peace.

Dissolving. Dissolving. Edges melting. Vast, luminous space, dissolving in space.

Shimmering clouds dissolving at the edge. Clouds dissolving in space. Dissipating. Dissolving. Merging in space.

Let go into that spaciousness. Hold nowhere. Let your heart merge in your own great fire.

Dissolving. Radiating into space. Merging with light. Dissolving in luminous space.

Let go into the light. In this vast luminosity is all that you have ever sought. Dissolving into the Great Heart.

Let go completely. Die gently into the light.

Floating free in vast space.

Let go of your knowing. Let go of your not knowing. All that comes to mind is old. Any thought is just old thought. Nothing to hold to.

"Just the simple fact of dying and the fact of the clear light."

Just the light entering the light.

Space within space.

No inside, no outside. Just am-ness. Edgeless being in endless space.

Dissolve into it. Floating free of the body, free of the mind. Merging in boundaryless space.

Space expanding into space. Dissolving into space. Floating in the vastness.

Peace. Mercy. Space.

And from across vast space notice now something gently approaching. It is the first breath of life.

Watch the breath approaching as if from far away. Experience it entering the body.

Each breath the first. Each inhalation the first breath of life.

Each breath completely new.

Each breath bringing us back into the body.

Taking birth once again.

Born back into the body.

Taking birth again to serve and be served. To learn. To teach. To care and be cared for.

Awareness once again entering the body as consciousness.

Pure awareness reinhabiting pure form. Birth.

Born again into the body. Each breath the first. Born again to bring mercy and healing to the injured world.

Taking birth for the benefit of all sentient beings.

Taking birth to heal.

The light body once again reanimating the heavy body. Each breath connecting, maintaining the light body within its momentary vehicle.

Once again the light clothes itself in form so as to act and to complete whatever healing remains.

Have mercy. Born again to the world. Born to bring

peace, to bring kindness. To bring healing to our pain and the pain of all sentient beings, unto the last blade of grass.

Born to learn, to be.

Each breath so precious, allowing us to stay a moment longer. Allowing us the healing we took birth for.

Born to take the teaching. Born to bring mercy.

May all beings coming and going know the peace of their own great nature. May all beings be free of suffering.

Let your eyes gently open.

Look around you. Here you are.

INTRODUCTION TO DEATH TRANSITION MEDITATION

The following guided meditation is inspired by the *Tibetan Book of the Dead* and similar texts. It is not offered as "what will be," but only as a worthwhile "scenario of investigation." Some have used this meditation to prepare for death or to help another prepare. Yet more have read it to loved ones after they left their body behind.

It is suggested that, more than just reading this meditation to one who is preparing for death or to one who has already died, one internalize these words by meditating on them. The support this practice provides then comes not from the intellectual mind but rather from the engaged heart.

This guidance through uncharted terrain becomes a tandem climb when two minds focus on the shared heart of being.

As you work/play with this meditation, remember that

this is not what death is like—this is what a meditation on death is like. The truth is a direct experience, not its reflection in concepts and words. It is in the palm of your hand. Let go and there it is. This meditation is a training in just such letting go. Mindfulness is the perfect preparation for this practice.

Make this material your own so that at the time of another's need it can come forth of itself. Let it pour from your heart. Let it come forth with your intuition and love. Trust that the loved one will find their way through with your compassion and encouragement.

If you intend to use this meditation with someone who has just died, it is suggested you start by absorbing and repeating in your heart the first few paragraphs or pages soon after death and continue that sharing during the next days as feels appropriate. Indeed, if you trust your intuitive sense of it all, you may wish to repeat, even several times a day, certain paragraphs that you sense might be useful. Just stay in loving contact and let the heart's connection share in harmony with that person's needs.

Let your concentration come from the heart, focused in concern for another's liberation. It is the heart energy that directs this meditation to another. Don't look into it paragraph by paragraph or word by word. Let it be the heart's rendition of what feels appropriate. Not simply reading it, but reminding oneself out loud and sharing that remembrance in ways that might be useful to open the heart and let go lightly. Allow yourself to amplify and expand on any of the meditation you sense is particularly useful for that individual. Make the heart connection the medium for a deeper love and trust of each person's original nature.

A GUIDED DEATH TRANSITION MEDITATION

(To be read very slowly to a friend or silently to oneself.)

Imagine that your body no longer has the strength, the energy, to maintain its connection with the life-force, with the body of awareness within. And imagine now that you are beginning to experience the process of dissolving out of that body. Slowly, the earth element begins to melt. The feeling of solidity falling away, melting into the water element, becoming a flowingness. The edges less defined. The water element dissolving, dissolving into the fire element. Sensations from the body no longer distinct, melting away, leaving just a spaciousness. Dissolving out of the body. Leaving that heavier form behind. Dissolving into consciousness itself. Just space floating in space.

My friend, listen now, for that which is called death has arrived. So let go gently, gently, of all that holds you back. Of all that pulls you away from this precious moment. Know that now you have arrived at the transition called death. Open to it. Let go into it.

318

Recognize the changing experience of the mind as it separates from the body, dissolving.

Dissolving now into the realms of pure light. Your true nature shining everywhere before you.

My friend, the clear light of your original nature is revealed now in this release from heavier form. Enter into the brilliance of the light. Approach it with reverence and compassion. Draw it into yourself and become what you have always been.

My friend, maintain an openheartedness, a spaciousness of being that does not grasp. Let things be as they are without the least attempt to interfere. Pushing away nothing. Grasping at nothing.

Enter the essential nature of your own being shining there before you, a great luminosity. Rest in being. Knowing it for what it is: this light shining, luminous before you is your own great nature.

My friend, at this moment your mind is pure luminous emptiness. Your original mind, the essence of being, shines before you. Its nature is compassion and love, vibrant and luminous.

This is the same light that shines from the open heart of Jesus. It is the pure light of the Buddha. It is the essential mind, inseparable luminosity and emptiness in the form of a great light. Holding to nothing, let go into this vastness. Dissolve into the light of your true being.

Let go, gently, gently, without the least force. Before you shines your true being. It is without birth, without death. It is the unborn and undying luminescence of being. It is an emanation of your Real Body. It is the immortal light shining in the eyes of newborns. Recognize this. It is the Ever-shining.

Let go of all which distracts or confuses the mind, all that created density in life. Let go into your undifferentiated nature shining there before you. You have always been this light now revealed.

Go gently into it. Let go of fear and bewilderment. Do not pull back from the immensity of your true being. Now is a moment for liberation.

Friend, listen very closely, for hearing these words as you pass through transition can liberate you from the clinging which has caused you such pain in the past.

These words can free you from the confusion that may arise from whatever illusion of separateness you held most precious in this life just passed.

Listen without distraction, for what is called death has occurred. You are not alone in leaving this world. It happens to everyone. Let go of the body you have just left behind. You cannot stay. Indeed, to attempt to force back into this life will only cause you to wander in bewilderment and confusion, stumbling in the ancient illusions of the mind. Painting wonders and creating terrors that are un-real. Open to the truth. Trust in your own great nature.

My friend, if the light should fade or if you should begin to feel faint, recognize whatever yearning pulls at you. Note it. Let it go. Release it into the unfolding process. And return your attention to the Great Light before you. It is the pure white light of pure being before old conditioning and fear divide it into separate images, thoughts, and personal preferences. This is the light of oneness, the underlying nature of all things.

Merge with it, letting go of all that has for so long kept you separate. This is the light whose pure reflection is the truth.

See the nature of the longings that shatter this oneness into the separate and fearful, experiencing as seemingly real the thousands of beautiful images and frightening images that the mind has carried for so long. Do not be confused or bewildered.

Recognize whatever object comes between you and the light to be only the empty projections of old mind, ema-nations of desire and yearning.

Now, reaching this wonder-filled moment, do not cling to either the peaceful or afflictive states of mind that you are familiar with from the past. Allow yourself mercifully to let go of whatever resistance might hold you back.

Now is the time to hold nowhere, to melt into the great light of your original nature. Dissolve into pure being.

Observe it all from the still point of the heart, wishing all the forms that appear before you the great joy of liberation as they arise and pass away.

Go forward. Let all that arises pass away as well.

See each image distinctly. Remember each to be only the projections of old mind, seemingly solid, seemingly existing outside of you. But they are just empty shadows. Dreams of mind accumulated through birth after birth.

Let nothing distract you. Let nothing draw you away from the light of your true nature.

My friend, when the body and mind separate, the clear light appears shining with such an intensity that old fears may cause you to withdraw, to attempt to escape its incredible brilliance.

Let go of fears or yearnings from the past. Let the heart navigate toward the natural radiance of being that shines before you. Recognize it. Enter into it.

A surprising sound may come from within this light, like thunder, or the rumbling of a train. This is the great sound of your original nature.

You no longer have the physical body which you may have often mistaken for your real body, the body of aware-ness, the light body now floating free. A shining body of awareness that experiences thoughts as though they were external objects. Be watchful of the unconscious tenden-cies, which throughout life have directed and driven you, creating painful realms of pleasure or fear when clarity was not present.

Know yourself to be pure edgeless awareness. The very

suchness of truth. Trust in this truth, let go of anything
that obscures it.

You have no physical body of flesh or blood; no sounds,
colors, lights, or mental creations can hurt you. Nothing
you have feared in the past can physically harm you.
Indeed, you cannot die, for what is called death has already
occurred to the body. Now you move through the realms
between births.

Let go of your old fear of bodily harm in these realms
beyond life. Though the body has fallen away, still the
mind may hold the fear of death. See the illusion of such
thoughts.

Old fears. Old bindings. Let go. Let go into the light.
Experiencing with openness and love the unfolding. Holding nowhere.

Dissolve into the light that seems to shine from the
sacred heart of Jesus, from the vast brow of Buddha, from
the open palm of Mary. Go into the light, go beyond
personifications of the truth into the shining truth itself.
Go beyond even the most beautiful or most frightening
mental projections.

Recognize the sounds, the lights as just states of mind.
See them as you would a flickering fire, ever-changing
shapes and forms, momentarily existent, then gone, of no
solidity, of no substance. Do not be afraid. Be drawn like a
moth to your great being, there, shining there before you.

My friend, if you are frightened or withdraw, you may
continue to wander on, separating the one into the many.
Forgetful of your own great nature.

If you are seduced by the images of your sexual desires
as they brush by, yearning for pleasure, you may be drawn
by duller lights into the shadows they create and become
forgetful of your own great light. Remember your deepest
truth and enter into it.

As time goes by, if feeings of anger or aggression arise,
attempting to guide you falsely, misdirecting you, recognize

them as obstructions to your essential freedom. Seeing their dense, afflictive nature, observe them like passing clouds that momentarily obscure the sun. And merge directly with this solar star.

Gently and with great compassion, remember the power of such feelings to draw the heart away from the light. Gently let go of all that obscures the vastness of being.

Know all thoughts, all sights, all feelings to be but the emanations of mind.

Let go of false knowing. Let go of old models and superstitions. Merge back fully with yourself. Open to the totality of being. All that is seen, is one with the mind. Melt into that oneness. Become the essence of all that is. Feel yourself beyond the mind's forms. Beyond form itself. No longer clinging to old addictions of pleasure and pain, let your mind go and rest in the pure light.

Beware of the power of old desires to drag you toward unconscious rebirth. Trust the heart's devotion to the truth.

Do not be wearied as you travel through these shining realms, perhaps so different from what you imagined. You are the essence of awareness itself.

Know yourself as awareness present in each moment of consciousness, experiencing as it does whatever arises.

If you should be attracted to old thoughts, visions of old friends, feelings that draw you toward old situations, know that all these are but the shadow play of the conditioned mind. Go beyond the conditioned into unconditional love. Merge with the light of your own great heart.

As time passes, if you feel pulled to take incarnation once again, choose carefully the birth that seems appropriate. The birth which encourages the truths you have discovered after death. Recall the essence of being so as not to be tossed headlong into a new birth without awareness. Stay awake and sharp. Allow your heart to navigate by the light of its own great compassion. Be altogether patient.

My friend, you see now that even death is impermanent. That who you are, awareness itself, does not depend upon a body gross or subtle, or even life or death, for its existence.

Rest in your supreme state, free from activity and care, free of separateness and fearing. Rest in the deathlessness of your great nature, free of judging, free of the duality that causes forgetfulness. Enter into the essential spaciousness of being. Dissolve into your own true nature, vast, luminous space.

Notice any tendency born of fear to attempt control and the painful contraction it can create. Take advantage of this most wonderful opportunity. Float free in the vast spaciousness. Your devotion to the truth will carry you through.

My friend, many days have passed now since you left your body. Now know the truth as it is and go on, taking refuge in the vastness of your original nature. Know that you are well guided by your compassion and love. You are the essence of all things. You are the light.

When I was attempting to create an applicable guided meditation from various translations of the *Tibetan Book of the Dead*, particularly aided by the Chogyam Trungpa and Freemantle rendition, there was much I did not understand about the text, its use, and the possibilities of altering it to fit the needs of the dying patients with whom I was working. Knowing that the "real thing" lived not far away, I sought out Lama Yeshe, a Tibetan Lama of the first magnitude, a wonderfully spacious collaborateur on the path, to request his review of what I was up to and answer a few questions. We laughed so hard we died.

This meditation is dedicated to Lama Yeshe, who helped so much with informed comprehension of the text and the heart to carry it off.

AFTERNOTE

When contemplating what may occur after life leaves the body, there is a tendency to believe that what is next encountered is the whole of the truth. That the light and possible scintillating afterworlds define the whole of us. But after all it must be remembered that all we are speaking of is the process of learning that takes on a body—that enters into form—in order to complete its healing into undifferentiated, unconditional suchness. To the greatest part of us, that enormity (which we seek), nothing much is happening. It is the ever uninjured and uninjurable, the unborn and deathless vastness of being. It is the space in which these incessant dramas of birth, aging, and death play themselves out until only the "heart which needs nothing more" remains and merges inseparably into the "*uh*" of its true nature.

We take birth to meet ourselves again in a world so ripped with pain we cannot miss the lesson. We take birth to learn to keep our heart open in hell. To perfect mercy and wisdom. And to remember that even these constantly turning cycles of birth and death, even these various bodies and worlds we inhabit, are happening only on a relatively dense level where physical and psychological laws predominate. And to discover that which is greater than even the subtlest body. It is the healing we took birth for. We dress for the occasion.

ABOUT THE AUTHOR

In the mid-1970s, while working with Ram Dass (*Grist for the Mill,* 1976) and teaching meditation in the California prison system, STEPHEN LEVINE met Elisabeth Kübler-Ross. For the next few years he led workshops with her and learned from the terminally ill the need for deeper levels of healing and profound joy of service (*A Gradual Awakening,* 1979). In 1980 he began teaching workshops with his wife, Ondrea, as they continued to serve the terminally ill and those deeply affected by loss as Co-Directors of the Hanuman Foundation Dying Project. (*Who Dies?,* 1982). For three years Ondrea and Stephen maintained a free-consultation telephone line for those confronting serious illness or the possible death of a loved one (*Meetings at the Edge,* 1984). As the Levines continued to gain insight from those who overcame illness and surpassed death, their explorations deepened while further meditative techniques were developed to "let the healing in". Their guided meditations for the healing of illness, grief holdings, heavy emotional states, and sexual abuse and subtler forms of life/death preparation brought them international recognition (*Healing into Life and Death,* 1987 and *Guided Meditations, Explorations and Healings,* 1992), having aided thousands of people worldwide. Presently Stephen and Ondrea Levine are living in the high mountains of the Southwest, "attempting to practise what we preach" in the silence of the deep woods. They are seeking the "healing we took birth for", working on a long-awaited new book, *Relationships as a Path to Awakening,* feeding the animals and the trees, and "examining the weatherbeaten out-croppings and the sun-dappled forests of the mind, sipping at the clear wellsprings of the heart".